Best wishes to my friend, Johnny !

Shirley Morrison

Encouraging Words

Redemption In Any Language

PHILLIP MORRISON

Copyright © 2020 Phillip Morrison.

All rights reserved. No part of this book may be used or reproduced by any means, graphic, electronic, or mechanical, including photocopying, recording, taping or by any information storage retrieval system without the written permission of the author except in the case of brief quotations embodied in critical articles and reviews.

This book is a work of non-fiction. Unless otherwise noted, the author and the publisher make no explicit guarantees as to the accuracy of the information contained in this book and in some cases, names of people and places have been altered to protect their privacy.

WestBow Press books may be ordered through booksellers or by contacting:

WestBow Press
A Division of Thomas Nelson & Zondervan
1663 Liberty Drive
Bloomington, IN 47403
www.westbowpress.com
844-714-3454

Because of the dynamic nature of the Internet, any web addresses or links contained in this book may have changed since publication and may no longer be valid. The views expressed in this work are solely those of the author and do not necessarily reflect the views of the publisher, and the publisher hereby disclaims any responsibility for them.

Any people depicted in stock imagery provided by Getty Images are models, and such images are being used for illustrative purposes only. Certain stock imagery © Getty Images.

ISBN: 978-1-6642-1163-6 (sc)
ISBN: 978-1-6642-1161-2 (hc)
ISBN: 978-1-6642-1162-9 (e)

Library of Congress Control Number: 2020921818

Print information available on the last page.

WestBow Press rev. date: 11/10/2020

Scripture quotations marked (NIV) are taken from the Holy Bible, New International Version®, NIV®. Copyright © 1973, 1978, 1984, 2011 by Biblica, Inc.® Used by permission of Zondervan. All rights reserved worldwide. www.zondervan.com The "NIV" and "New International Version" are trademarks registered in the United States Patent and Trademark Office by Biblica, Inc.®

Scripture marked (KJV) taken from the King James Version of the Bible.

Scripture marked (ASV) taken from the American Standard Version of the Bible.

Scripture quotations marked (CEV) are from the Contemporary English Version Copyright © 1991, 1992, 1995 by American Bible Society, Used by Permission.

Scripture marked (NASB) taken from the New American Standard Bible (NASB) Copyright ©1960, 1962, 1963, 1968, 1971, 1972, 1973, 1975, 1977, 1995 by The Lockman Foundation, La Habra, CA. All rights reserved. Used by Permission. www.lockman.org.

Scripture quotations marked (NLT) are taken from the Holy Bible, New Living Translation, copyright ©1996, 2004, 2015 by Tyndale House Foundation. Used by permission of Tyndale House Publishers, a Division of Tyndale House Ministries, Carol Stream, Illinois 60188. All rights reserved.

Scripture marked (BSB) taken from the Holy Bible, Berean Study Bible, BSB Copyright ©2016, 2018 by Bible Hub Used by Permission. All Rights Reserved Worldwide.

Scripture quotations marked MSG are taken from THE MESSAGE, copyright © 1993, 2002, 2018 by Eugene H. Peterson. Used by permission of NavPress. All rights reserved. Represented by Tyndale House Publishers, a Division of Tyndale House Ministries.

Scripture quotations marked CSB have been taken from the Christian Standard Bible®, Copyright © 2017 by Holman Bible Publishers. Used by permission. Christian Standard Bible® and CSB® are federally registered trademarks of Holman Bible Publishers.

DEDICATION

Thanking all the people who helped make this book possible would require much more than a page, but I thank them all. Special thanks to Ron Thweatt, who taught me everything I know about printing, and to Joel Butts, outstanding graphic artist who designed this book.

This volume is gratefully dedicated to the memory of Mary Margaret Grounds Morrison, my wife for more than sixty-one years, who was my inspiration, my love, and my life.

ENDORSEMENTS

Phillip Morrison uses humankind – our history, our geography, and our stories – to unveil a deep longing we have for Redemption. He reminds us that true Redemption is more than a word to describe our pursuit of goodness. The Father offers Redemption that revealed our brokenness, cost a life, and released us from the power of sin and death. This book reveals that Redemption.
—Dr. Damon Cathey, Executive Principal, Metro Nashville Public School.

Phillip Morrison has enjoyed a full life as Christian minister, pastor, counselor, writer, editor, husband, father, and grandfather. He is a keen observer of diverse real-world experiences, and is a deep, reflective thinker. With open mind and gentle spirit, Phillip has blessed thousands with both his speaking and writing, especially his "Encouraging Words" emails. In this collection of several of these writings, readers will receive rich insights and strong encouragement for the living of these days.
—Dr. Perry C. Cotham, retired university professor, pulpit minister, and author of numerous books, including "One World/Many Neighbors" and "American Rhetorical Excellence".

If you have read any of Phillip's "Encouraging Words," you have come away feeling blessed and lifted. As a minister of the gospel, his words provide a unique spiritual perspective designed to encourage self-reflection. Transparency about his personal life – successes, failures, and disappointments – will produce flashes of fond memories in your own life. This book will remind you of the blessings you have been given by God and cause you to share them with others.

—*Joseph Tucker, Elder, Church of Christ in Falls Church, Virginia and President of Alpha Printing.*

FOREWORD

I wasn't born with printer's ink in my blood, but I loved books almost from infancy. The first book I owned, before I was old enough for school, was a small volume of Bible stories. Soon, with the guidance of Mrs. Latimer, librarian in our small town, I had read almost all the children's books and as many of the adult books as she thought appropriate.

By the time I got to seventh grade, I was editing the Bulldog Gazette, a role that continued in high school. My favorite after-school-hangout place was Byrd Cain's print shop where he was owner, publisher, and editor of the weekly Old Hickory News. Mine was strictly a volunteer role as I was too young to have a job. Under Mr. Cain's tutelage, I learned to handset headlines while he ran the clunky old linotype. I can still read headlines upside down and backward, and I still know how to keep my hands out of an old "finger smasher" press.

My friend, teacher, mentor, and idol, Batsell Barrett Baxter, asked me years later to be his hands and feet to develop a magazine for respondents to the Herald of Truth radio and television programs. I jumped at the opportunity to help birth "UpReach" magazine and, still later, "Wineskins" magazine in partnership with Rubel Shelly and Mike Cope.

Due to age and infirmities, Mary Margaret and I moved to Austin in 2011 to live near one of our daughters. Despite knowing that I could no longer stand and preach, I still felt the call of God on my life. Remembering that the thousands of people I had known in sixty years of ministry all needed encouragement, I began writing and circulating a weekly essay called Encouraging Words. Almost from the beginning, people began asking me to compile some of those writings in a book, and this little volume is the result. Other volumes may follow, even if my children have to publish them posthumously!

After Mary Margaret died, I wandered in such a fog that I suffered several falls, one of which caused an almost fatal broken neck. After months of surgery, rehab, and recovery, I finally got back to my computer only to discover that I couldn't remember how to do the simplest task. Frequent calls to children and grandchildren began, "How do I...?" Those calls are still being made, though not so often.

As you read this and volumes that follow, I thank you and send you this simple message from I Thessalonians 5:11 – "Encourage one another."

~ *Phillip Morrison*

CONTENTS

Endorsements ix
Foreword... xi

Chapter 1   Redemption in any Language..........................1
Chapter 2   Making Peace and Making War 5
Chapter 3   And God Saw that it was Good........................9
Chapter 4   Have I Got a Deal for You!............................13
Chapter 5   The Land of Beginning Again........................17
Chapter 6   A Holiday Few Remember.............................21
Chapter 7   Watching You, Watching You!......................25
Chapter 8   Leading from Behind 29
Chapter 9   Pay it Forward 33
Chapter 10   Catching Flies...37
Chapter 11   Run… Walk… Crawl… Finish!.......................41
Chapter 12   It Is Finished!..45
Chapter 13   He Is Risen Indeed!.......................................49
Chapter 14   Red to Honor, White to Remember................53
Chapter 15   Broken Hearts and Living Spirits 57
Chapter 16   Blessed Are the Dead Who Die in the Lord ...61
Chapter 17   Stop by the Lobby and See my Underwear....65
Chapter 18   It Is Well with my Soul..................................69
Chapter 19   Well, I Love You Too! 73
Chapter 20   I Don't Even Buy Green Bananas!.................77
Chapter 21   He's with Me 81
Chapter 22   The Water Is Your Friend!............................85

Chapter 23	Daughter of the World	89
Chapter 24	Shame in Black and White	93
Chapter 25	Mine's Got a Popsicle in It!	97
Chapter 26	It's an Absolute Joy!	101
Chapter 27	By the Grace of God	105
Chapter 28	My Certainty for Your Uncertainty?	109
Chapter 29	Beauty Is not Always Pretty	113
Chapter 30	When America Became a Church	117
Chapter 31	You've Got a Lifetime Guarantee!	121
Chapter 32	Are You Ready for Some Football?	125
Chapter 33	My Life My Argument	129
Chapter 34	If Necessary, Use Words	133
Chapter 35	The Man up Yonder Does Forgive	137
Chapter 36	God was There Every Single Time	141
Chapter 37	A Smudge on Your Forehead	145
Chapter 38	The Things of First Importance	149
Chapter 39	Blessed Assurance, Jesus Is Mine	153
Chapter 40	I Will Never Leave you nor Forsake you	157

CHAPTER ONE

Redemption in any Language

> *On top of ... Corcovado Mountain ... stands the 98-foot-tall Cristo Redentor, Christ the Redeemer statue, arms outstretched in both invitation and assurance of the constant presence and protection of Jesus."*

Approximately half of the almost eight billion people in the world watched television from Brazil four years ago when both the World Cup and the 2016 Summer Olympics were contested in Brazil. A few years before that, Mary Margaret and I visited Brazil on a more significant mission. Although preoccupied with getting acquainted with our first grandchild, we still had some time to visit famous attractions, including the iconic Cristo Redentor statue overlooking Rio de Janeiro.

> *The mansions on the hilltops, some with their own helipads and cantilevered access roads, and the cardboard shanties alike all contain people needing redemption."*

On top of the 2,300 foot Corcovado Mountain overlooking the city, on a huge pedestal reaching another 26 feet into the sky, stands the 98-foot-tall Cristo Redentor, Christ the Redeemer statue, arms outstretched in both invitation and assurance of the constant presence and protection of Jesus. Constructed of concrete and steel, and clad in triangular soapstone tiles, the statue has protection from the weather not including the frequent lightning strikes.

As is often the case with national monuments, this one was planned for a long time before it was actually built. Since the 1850s, there had been several attempts to agree on a design and location, but the actual construction didn't begin until 1922, and the monument opened on October 12, 1931. In 2007, the statue was officially named one of the Seven Wonders of the Modern World.

Thousands of tourists were in Brazil for the World Cup and the Olympics, and many of them joined other thousands who already waited in line for hours to ride the 2.3 mile cog railway up the mountain or brave the hairpin curves of the road winding through the Tijuca Forest National Park. The view from the top of Corcovado makes the wait and the trip more than worthwhile. Spread out before a gawker is one of the great cities of the world with a population of 6.5 million in Rio proper and a total population of perhaps 18 million, depending on how large an area one wants to include.

The waters of Guanabara Bay, punctuated by Sugarloaf Mountain, and bordered by the famed Copacabana and Ipanema Beaches all provide photo ops hardly matched anywhere else in the world. Not so visible are the 763 slums or favelas where poverty, crime, disease, and squalor of every kind make up the Rio not found on travel posters.

Over this city of extreme wealth and indescribable poverty

stands Christ the Redeemer, arms open in invitation by day and by night, reminding, calling, and inviting. The mansions on the hilltops, some with their own helipads and cantilevered access roads, and the cardboard shanties alike all contain people needing redemption.

> *Redeeming a laundered shirt is routine; redeeming a lost soul is profound."*

I was reminded of the word redemption when the Jewish woman at the laundry displayed the number tattooed on her arm to honor the grandmother imprisoned at Auschwitz, called me by name and said, "You don't need your ticket, what do you think this is, no tickee no shirtee?" We agreed that I hadn't heard that, and she hadn't said that in a long time, but we both had heard the saying all our lives. We also agreed that it was uncalled for and unappreciated ethnic slang we would do well to forget. But I couldn't forget the nagging question of how that saying began.

A little research led me to a University of Idaho study that found the saying probably began in the 1800s when Chinese immigrants began moving to the west coast of the United States to work on major projects like the intercontinental railroad and establish restaurants, laundries, and other service businesses. Not speaking English, they developed what the Idaho researchers called English Pidgin Chinese. To be sure they got the right clothes back to their rightful owners, they gave claim checks or tickets that had to be presented when the laundry was redeemed. The researchers further discovered that an animated movie short in 1921 had popularized the saying, as had a Little Rascals episode in 1934 and several other films in the 1930s and 40s.

The redemption theme was carried out in literature by a Leo Tolstoy play and a Leon Uris novel. In the music world it caught the attention of performers from Johnny Cash to Bob Marley. The idea that we need to reclaim something already owned fascinates thoughtful people of any language or culture.

Redeeming a laundered shirt is routine; redeeming a lost soul is profound. The Apostle Paul seemed to be searching for just the right word when he described Jesus as "wisdom from God – that is, our righteousness, holiness and redemption" (1 Corinthians 1:30, NIV). I can redeem my shirts with a piece of paper or a plastic card, but "it was not with perishable things such as silver or gold that you were redeemed... but with the precious blood of Christ..." (1 Peter 1:18, 19, NIV).

The outstretched arms of Cristo Redentor reach 92 feet from fingertip to fingertip, but the outstretched arms of Christ the Redeemer reach to infinity, embracing all who will come.

CHAPTER TWO

Making Peace and Making War

> *Soldiers on both sides expected to be home by Christmas that year, never dreaming that the war would last four years and claim almost ten million lives."*

An event that occurred a hundred years ago is retold in some form during every Christmas season. But current events make me remember this story more often.

Periodically, the Israeli Defense Force and a group of Hamas-led Arab terrorists renew an intense war in a tiny strip of land known as Gaza. Only about eight miles wide and thirty-five miles long, Gaza is home to almost two million people. Although we are more familiar with current wars, the conflict between Arabs and Jews began with Ishmael and Isaac, both sons of Abraham, 4,000 years ago.

During less than a month of recent fighting, at least 1,600 Palestinians, many of them children, were killed and almost 6,000 were injured. Sixty-six Israelis were killed. Five cease-fire agreements have been reached, and all five have been violated.

A seventy-two-hour cease-fire lasted just an hour and twenty minutes before a Hamas suicide bomber killed himself and two Israeli soldiers, and another Israeli soldier was apparently captured.

> *The spirit of goodwill continued far into the night and spread along the Western Front until an estimated 100,000 men were observing the informal truce."*

A hundred years ago, what we now call World War I began on July 28, 1914. Soldiers on both sides expected to be home by Christmas that year, never dreaming that the war would last four years and claim almost ten million lives. In today's high-tech wars, soldiers drop bombs and fire long-range weapons that kill people they never see. A hundred years ago, war was soldier against soldier, often in a hand-to-hand struggle to the death.

As daylight faded on Christmas Eve, 1914, soldiers on both sides were sad that they would miss Christmas at home. German troops were in their trenches and British troops in theirs, separated in places by only thirty yards of "No-Man's Land."

Suddenly the British soldiers heard a familiar melody and realized that the Germans were singing "Stille Nacht" ("Silent Night"). The Brits answered with "O Come, All Ye Faithful," and soon a German offered a bottle of wine to any British soldier willing to venture into No-Man's Land to accept it. The challenge was met by a Brit who took a cake from the Christmas box he had received from home and stepped out to make the exchange. Before long the neutral zone was filled with German and British soldiers, exchanging food and cigarettes, and singing carols.

> *And many peoples shall come, and say: 'Come; let us go up to the mountain of the Lord, to the house of the God of Jacob, that he may teach us his ways and that we may walk in his paths.' For out of Zion shall go the law, and the word of the Lord from Jerusalem. He shall judge between the nations, and shall decide disputes for many peoples; and they shall beat their swords into plowshares, and their spears into pruning hooks; nation shall not lift up sword against nation, neither shall they learn war anymore." (Isaiah 2; 3-4, KJV)*

The spirit of goodwill continued far into the night and spread along the Western Front until an estimated 100,000 men were observing the informal truce. In a letter, one German soldier described the cease-fire as "a day of peace in war.... It is only a pity that it was not decisive peace."

On Christmas Day impromptu soccer games were played, including a legendary one between the 133rd Royal Saxon Regiment and some Scottish troops wearing tartan kilts. Somebody produced a real ball to replace the corned beef tins others were kicking, goals were marked by helmets placed on the ground, and a real match was described by Lt. Johannes Niemann of the German side.

His fellow-soldiers roared, he reported, "when a gust of wind revealed that the Scots wore no drawers under their kilts."

> *Snoopy's Christmas" has Snoopy and The Red Baron halting their private war long enough to honor the season.*

In 2004, Alfred Anderson, the last surviving British soldier, 108 years old, related how each British soldier had received Christmas greetings from seventeen-year-old Princess Mary, including an embossed brass box filled with cigarettes. After Alfred gave away all his smokes during the Christmas Eve truce, he found that the New Testament his mother had given him fit perfectly in the brass box where he kept it until the war was over.

The Christmas truce of 1914 was the inspiration for Paul McCartney's 1983 video, "Pipes of Peace" and for the 1996 movie, *A Midnight Clear*. Even "Snoopy's Christmas" has Snoopy and The Red Baron halting their private war long enough to honor the season.

In Stanley Weintraub's 2001 book *Silent Night: The Story of the World War I Christmas Truce*, he says the truce "remains a symbol of hope to those who believe that recognition of our common humanity may someday reverse the maxim that 'Peace Is Harder to Make than War.'"

CHAPTER THREE

And God Saw that it was Good

> "A horrible year was salvaged – redeemed, some would say – by the successful space mission called Apollo 8."

1968 was a bad year in America. Right out of the box, January saw the Vietnam War take another disastrous turn as the Tet Offensive caused the deaths of more than a thousand Americans and South Vietnamese in just two weeks. In February, the Kerner Commission reported that "our nation is moving toward two societies, one black, one white – separate and unequal." In March, American soldiers were accused of killing more than 400 Vietnamese civilians in a far-away village called My Lai. On April 4, Dr. Martin Luther King, Jr., 39, was assassinated while standing on a hotel balcony in Memphis. On June 5, Robert F. Kennedy, 42, was assassinated in Los Angeles just minutes after delivering a victory speech following the Democratic primary.

> *As Anders, Borman, and Lovell emerged from the backside of the Moon and saw the earth hanging like a bright ornament in the sky – the picture would later be captioned Earthrise – they took turns reading the first words from the first book of the Bible."*

A horrible year was salvaged – redeemed, some would say – by the successful space mission called Apollo 8. Astronauts William Anders, Frank Borman, and Jim Lovell became the first human beings to orbit the Moon and see things never before seen by human eyes. They were the first of only twenty-four people who have left our planet and gone to the Moon.

Fifty-two years ago, at 7:51 EST, a mighty Saturn V rocket carrying its first human cargo, lifted off from Cape Canaveral, Florida to begin a historic journey that would last 146 hours, 59 minutes, and 49 seconds. After a journey of approximately three days, the Apollo capsule entered lunar orbit, and would make ten orbits before returning to earth on December 27.

> *Jim Lovell said, 'I realized how insignificant we all are if everything I'd ever known is behind my thumb.'"*

It was during the ninth orbit of the Moon that Anders, Borman, and Lovell sent a priceless Christmas Eve gift back to earth. As they emerged from the backside of the Moon, they photographed the earth, hanging like a bright ornament in the sky.

The picture would later be captioned Earthrise – they took turns reading the first words from the first book of the Bible:

> *In the beginning ...*
> *God created the heavens and the earth. And the earth was without form, and void; and darkness*

was upon the face of the deep. And the spirit of God moved upon the face of the waters. And God said, Let there be light: and there was light. And God saw the light, that it was good: and God divided the light from the darkness. And God called the light Day, and the Darkness he called Night. And the evening and the morning were the first day. And God said, Let there be a firmament in the midst of the waters, and let it divide the waters from the waters. And God made the firmament and divided the waters which were under the firmament from the waters which were above the firmament: and it was so. And God called the firmament Heaven. And the evening and the morning were the second day. And God said, Let the waters under the heaven be gathered together unto one place, and let the dry land appear: and it was so. And God called the dry land Earth; and the gathering together of the waters He called the Seas:
… and God saw that it was good."
(Genesis 1:1-10, KJV)

> *We came all this way to explore the Moon, and the most important thing is that we discovered the Earth."*

When Tom Brokaw wrote *Boom!* (his account of the 1960s) he saw this voyage and reading as bright hours in an otherwise disastrous year. When he interviewed Jim Lovell, the former astronaut, he found him still in awe as he remembered: "At one point I sighted the earth with my thumb – and my thumb from that distance fit over the entire planet. I realized how insignificant we all are if everything I'd ever known is behind my thumb."

> "We're all astronauts on this spaceship Earth – about six or seven billion of us – and we have to work and live together."

Frank Borman said, "We came all this way to explore the Moon, and the most important thing is that we discovered the Earth."

Lovell remembers the people who sent messages from all around the globe, saying, "Thank you for saving 1968." "When you see Earth from the Moon," Lovell says, "you realize how fragile it is and just how limited the resources are. We're all astronauts on this spaceship Earth – about six or seven billion of us – and we have to work and live together."

To echo the closing words of Mission Commander Borman: "And from the crew of Apollo 8, we close with good night, good luck, a Merry Christmas, and God bless all of you on the Good Earth."

CHAPTER FOUR

Have I Got a Deal for You!

> " You can forget about the price of gasoline because the Tesla is all-electric!"

Assuming you haven't already finished your Christmas shopping by camping out and hoping to be first through the mall doors on Black Friday, have I got a deal for you! You've probably missed out on the Neiman Marcus special edition Aston Martin Vanquish Volante, as they only made ten and have been taking orders at $344,500 each since October 23. (For the more ordinary folks, the Neiman Marcus Chevy Camaro convertible special sold all 100 available units in just three minutes in 2010.)

For all you losers, may I recommend a Tesla? You never heard of a Tesla? I'm not surprised, as they only make a few thousand a year. However, you could be the first on your street to own this car. It gets rave reviews from auto experts. The plain-Jane version costs $70,000 and the "nicely equipped" version goes for $96,000. And you can forget about the price of gasoline because the Tesla is all-electric! So, jump in your new S-model, and enjoy the quietest, most luxurious ride ever – for about 250 miles. Then you'll have to stop for a minimum five-hour recharge – assuming you run out of juice near a recharging station. For 96 grand, shouldn't you at least be able to make it to the state line? Maine to California would take – driving four hours, recharging five hours – forget it. Maybe they should offer a long extension cord as an extra.

> *Will Christmas really be a failure if retail sales are down a bit from last year?"*

If 42-year-old billionaire Elon Musk can't sell you a Tesla, he'd like to put you in a vacuum tube (a larger version of the one that whisks your bank deposit to the teller inside) and send you around the country at 760 miles per hour. If you've ever used PayPal, he's already affected your life, and he'd like to talk to you about solar energy, space travel, and who knows what else.

There is something fundamentally flawed about an economy based on spending and consumption. Will Christmas really be a failure if retail sales are down a bit from last year? Is larger credit-card debt really a sign of prosperity?

When I think about the wish-list cars, I remember my mother talking about the first automobile she ever saw. When a T-model Ford went down the country road near their farmhouse, she and her siblings ran to the road to smell the tracks. Not so unreasonable when you consider that the more familiar horse-drawn buggies certainly left a tell-tale odor. My brother and I would just roll our eyes in disbelief when Mother and Daddy would talk about growing up in the Great Depression years when they were lucky to get an orange and a homemade toy for Christmas gifts.

The deal I have for you has nothing to do with luxury cars or door-busting sales, and everything to do with serving others. How would your Christmas look if it didn't involve conspicuous consumption? When I assumed a December identity involving a white beard and a red suit, I had to work hard to avoid becoming part of a system I didn't really like.

> " I did all the shopping myself, wrapped all the gifts myself, and I just had to put them under the tree all by myself."

Surely there is more to Christmas than memorizing toy catalogs so Santa can pretend to know all about the latest must-haves. I loved the kids but hated dealing with over-bearing parents who expected Santa to be the ultimate disciplinarian. The parents who threaten their children (If you don't be good, Santa Claus won't come to see you!) are sure to get a lecture and maybe even a lump of coal from this Santa.

How would your Christmas look if it didn't revolve around you? Being Santa is fun; being a Secret Santa is even more fun. The first year we had the Christmas Wish Tree at church, I tried to help a woman who was struggling to climb the steps with her arms full of packages. "No!" she barked, "I'll do it myself!" I made the same offer to help a few minutes later when I saw her with a second load and got the same reaction. She looked for me later and apologized with tears in her eyes. "I've never done anything like this," she explained, "but when I saw the Christmas Wish Tree at church it touched me like the one at the mall never did. I took one name, then another, and another, paying attention to ages and sizes. Then I did all the shopping myself, wrapped all the gifts myself, and I just had to put them under the tree all by myself. I hope you understand why I couldn't let you help!" I don't remember if I said anything, but I do remember hugging her real tight. Understand? Of course, I understood, and that was even before I was Santa!

Being a blessing to someone else, young, or old, is a deal you can't afford to miss!

" Death reveals that the world is not as it should be, but that it stands in need of redemption. Christ alone is the conquering of death" (Dietrich Bonhoeffer).

CHAPTER FIVE

The Land of Beginning Again

> "We finally flip the page, only to spend several weeks trying to remember how to write the New Year's date."

The new calendar made it look so simple. There are thirty-one neat squares for December and thirty-one neat squares for January. Just flip the page and ring in the New Year. In practice, however, it takes more than a month to flip the page. We start before Thanksgiving winding down the old year. There are lists of things to do before the old year ends, lists of the favorite this and the most popular that. There are predictions of what the New Year will bring, and explanations of why the predictions made last year did or didn't come true. Of course, we need a list of hangover cures for those who fail to understand that avoiding a hangover is the best cure of all.

We finally flip the page, only to spend several weeks trying to remember how to write the New Year's date.

> *Surely no one will predict a novel virus that will terrorize us for months!"*

Again, this year we are sure to read predictions that a giant asteroid may obliterate the earth, or that nuclear holocaust may vaporize us, or that an unseen black hole may suck our entire universe into its irresistible gravity. Surely no one will predict a novel virus that will terrorize us for months!

As I have listened to the recaps of last year's news stories, I have thought that the biggest news story of all time won't have anybody to report it. No jumbo headlines, no satellite TV images, no magazine special issues, not even any tweets. There will be no talking heads and no listening heads, for it will all happen "in the twinkling of an eye" (1 Corinthians 15:52, NIV). There will be no need or opportunity to analyze the story, for we'll all be part of the story.

The apostle Paul paints a beautiful picture of the life beyond, of the Christian assurance of resurrection (1 Thessalonians 4: 13-18, NIV). Critics of Christianity sometimes take what we think is beautiful and dismiss it as "pie in the sky by and by." We do look forward to future resurrection and the beginning of our new life, but we witness resurrection and new beginnings every day.

In my family of faith there is a woman who has overcome the demons of childhood sexual abuse and adult sexual addiction to build a new life in Christ. In addition to experiencing personal resurrection, she now helps other victims realize that they also can have new life.

Of course, the worry lines are still in her face and the scars are forever etched on her heart. The Great Physician specializes in genuine healing, not cosmetic surgery.

In my family of faith there is a man who, as a teenager, declared himself to be an atheist. More than three decades later, he tearfully reclaimed and proclaimed his faith in God. A brilliant man of science, he'll tell you that nothing he knows is as important as what he believes. He'll also tell you that resurrection to new life is much more than anticipation of the future.

In my family of faith there is me. Committed from childhood to a life of Christian service, I have faltered and fallen time and time again. But each time I have felt the gentle touch of Jesus as he picked me up, gave me new strength, and set my feet once again on my homeward way.

At the last day, the sound of God's trumpet will be heard throughout all the earth, and this time the shout of God's angels will be heard far beyond the borders of Bethlehem. What a day of rejoicing that will be!

When I first saw these lines from Louisa Fletcher many years ago, they quickly became favorites:

I wish that ...
there were some wonderful place
Called the Land of Beginning Again.
Where all our mistakes and all our heartaches
And all of our poor selfish grief
Could be dropped like a shabby old coat
at the door
... And never be put on again.

There is such a wonderful place, both here and now, and in the sweet by and by. Early in this New Year is a good time to make a new beginning, both for this year and for all the years to come.

> *In him we have redemption through his blood, the forgiveness of sins, in accordance with the riches of God's grace" (Ephesians 1:7, NIV).*

CHAPTER SIX

A Holiday Few Remember

> *The Four Chaplains quickly began to restore calm, escort the troops to the top deck, and see that they had life jackets and a place in the lifeboats."*

There is a national holiday that few remember and fewer celebrate. I'm referring to Four Chaplains Day, memorializing an event that occurred 77 years ago, on February 3, 1943. Shortly after midnight, the USAT Dorchester, with 904 troops and crew aboard, was torpedoed by a German submarine off the coast of Newfoundland. Only 230 of those aboard survived, with most of the casualties dying of hypothermia.

> *Just 18 minutes elapsed from the time the torpedo struck until the Dorchester went down."*

George L. Fox lied about his age to enlist in the Army during WWI where he was awarded several medals, including the Purple Heart, the Silver Star, and the French Croix de Guerre. He was ordained a Methodist minister in 1934, and reentered the Army as a Chaplain in 1942, assigned to duty at Camp Davis in North Carolina.

Alexander D. Goode was a Jewish Rabbi and the son of a Rabbi. He was educated at Hebrew Union College and earned the Ph. D. at Johns Hopkins University. He was turned down when he applied to be a Chaplain in the Navy, but after Pearl Harbor he volunteered as an Army Chaplain.

Clark V. Poling was the son of a Baptist minister who was also a Chaplain and was himself a minister in the Reformed Church of America. Educated at Yale Divinity School, he volunteered as an Army Chaplain because he wanted to face the same dangers other men were facing. He served at Camp Shelby in Hattiesburg, Mississippi before being assigned to duty in Europe.

John P. Washington, a Catholic priest from Newark, New Jersey, was educated at Seton Hall and Immaculate Conception Seminary. He was serving a parish in Elizabeth, New Jersey before being assigned to duty at Ft. Meade, Maryland.

When the Dorchester, originally a cruise ship designed to carry 400 passengers and crew, was torpedoed, many troops were trapped below decks and confusion reigned. The torpedo attack occurred at 12:55 a.m., knocking out the ship's electrical system and producing total darkness below deck. The Four Chaplains quickly began to restore calm, escort the troops to the top deck, and see that they had life jackets and a place in the lifeboats. When the life jackets were all gone, the four men took off their own jackets and gave them to the troops.

> *Petty Officer John Mahoney survived and recalled that when he started back to his quarters to get his gloves, Chaplain Goode said, 'I have an extra pair;*

take these.' Mahoney later realized that Goode didn't have extra gloves."

When last seen, they were standing arm-in-arm, saying prayers, and singing hymns as they went down with the ship. All four were First Lieutenants, newly graduated from Army Chaplain School at Harvard, and on their way to their first European assignments. All were awarded the Purple Heart posthumously but were denied the Medal of Honor on the technicality that they were not under fire while performing their heroic deeds.

The Four Chaplains took seriously these words of Jesus:

> Greater love has no one than this, that he lay down his life for his friends" (John 15:13 NIV).

Or, in the words of The Message, "Put your life on the line for your friends." Just 18 minutes elapsed from the time the torpedo struck until the Dorchester went down. I can only imagine the words exchanged by the Four Chaplains during that brief time. Or maybe there wasn't much conversation, just a shared awareness of the sacrifice they were called to make.

Petty Officer John Mahoney survived and recalled that when he started back to his quarters to get his gloves, Chaplain Goode said, "I have an extra pair; take these." Mahoney later realized that Goode didn't have an extra pair.

Stained glass windows commemorating their sacrifice are in the chapel at West Point, the Pentagon, and other U. S. military posts. The Immortal Chaplains Foundation was established in 1997 by relatives of the chaplains, survivors from the Dorchester, and crewmen from U-223, the German U-boat that fired the torpedo. The Foundation's goal "is to further the cause of unity without uniformity ... and to remind us of the capacity for compassion we all have within us, no matter the differences of race, religion or creed." The capacity for compassion we all have within us – encouraging words indeed.

On February 3, 1951, President Truman dedicated the Chapel of the Four Chaplains in the basement of Grace Baptist Church in Philadelphia: "This interfaith shrine… will stand through long generations to teach Americans that as men can die heroically as brothers so should they live together in mutual faith and goodwill."

Two Protestant pastors, a Rabbi, and a priest. I remember those heroes when I look in the mirror, and wonder....

CHAPTER SEVEN

Watching You, Watching You!

> *Following tradition, when he made the parachute team he acquired a discreetly placed tattoo with a small parachute and the number 288, signifying that he was the 288th cadet in the fifty-year history of the Academy to make the Wings of Blue team."*

Sometimes the dots just can't be connected. Or maybe I just don't know how to connect them. Or maybe they don't need to be connected.

In 1917, twenty-two-year-old Ernest Howard Discher left his engineering studies at the University of Detroit to answer a patriotic call to duty in World War I by enlisting in the U. S. Army. Because of his college work, he was commissioned a Lieutenant, assigned clerical duties, and then made an artillery spotter. When the war ended, he was being trained to go up in the rickety wood and canvas airplanes of the day to observe and report the trajectory of the enemy's artillery shells.

> *About all I know about #288 is that I like it better than #666."*

Returning to his hometown of Wheeling, West Virginia, he began arduously courting Florence Hannahs. They married over the strong objections of his Roman Catholic and her Church of Christ families, forming a union that would last 72 years. Their daughter, Dorothy Anne, attended David Lipscomb College where she met and married Mack Wayne Craig. When Florence's sister died, she left two babies who went to live with the Dischers as their own daughters. Phyllis, just over a year old, died at age twelve, and Mary Margaret, the newborn, became my wife after we met at college twenty-two years later.

Ernie became City Engineer for Wheeling, then Vice President and later President of a wholesale heating and plumbing supply company. Always a patriot, his World War I uniform would come out of the garment bag so he could wear it proudly on special holidays. His life was saved in 1948 by a young surgeon recently returned from World War II. At a time when radical surgery for colon cancer was almost unknown, Bill Hershey performed the operation that let Ernie live another 45 years.

Fast forward to 2003 when Florida Senator Bill Nelson appointed one of our grandsons to the U. S. Air Force Academy. Joe thrived in that environment and graduated near the top of his class in 2007. He became a member of the elite sky-diving team, the Wings of Blue, where his precision team won numerous competitions while at the Academy. Following tradition, when he made the parachute team he acquired a discreetly placed tattoo with a small parachute and the number 288, signifying that he was the 288th cadet in the fifty-year history of the Academy to make the Wings of Blue team.

Before Joe's first deployment to Afghanistan, Mary Margaret

decided he should be the one to have his great granddaddy's World War I uniform. He and his mom took it out of the storage bag one day so he could examine it thoroughly. Bryn said that Joe suddenly became very quiet, turned pale, and just pointed. He had turned the uniform pants inside out, and there, on the fabric forming the watch pocket, was the number 288, hidden for nearly a century.

> " At that time in my life I had an inordinate fear of God. I just knew God was keeping a record of every time I said a bad word, or every time I looked at a pretty girl, and especially the time I lied to Mrs. Philpot, my third-grade teacher."

When Joe asked me what I thought, I replied half seriously, "I think it means Ernie Discher's guardian angel is riding on your shoulder!" Lieutenant Discher #288, meet Lieutenant Kreidel #288, born 90 years and who knows how many wars apart. Two soldiers, two numbers, an unsolved mystery. About all I know about #288 is that I like it better than #666.

As I tried to find meaning in what logic tells me is a remarkable coincidence, I kept remembering a church song from my childhood. I can still hear those shrill voices: "Watching youuu, watching you; there's an all-seeing eye watching you." At that time in my life I had an inordinate fear of God. I just knew God was keeping a record of every time I said a bad word, or every time I looked at a pretty girl, and especially the time I lied to Mrs. Philpot, my third-grade teacher. I dreaded the day when God would pull out a long list of my sins and demand that I explain each and every one.

But what if the all-seeing eye is not there to condemn us but to protect us and guide us? What if there are guardian angels, or other representatives of God's love and care? A very public sinner who could have been stoned to death, instead heard encouraging words from Jesus himself after her accusers drifted away:

> 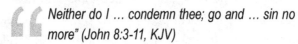 *Neither do I ... condemn thee; go and ... sin no more" (John 8:3-11, KJV)*

CHAPTER EIGHT

Leading from Behind

> " *The society which scorns excellence in plumbing as a humble activity and tolerates shoddiness in philosophy because it is an exalted activity will have neither good plumbing nor good philosophy; neither its pipes nor its theories will hold water."*

While watching the movie *Lincoln* and reading Doris Kearns Goodwin's book *Team of Rivals* on which the movie is based, I was reminded that we often see the past through rose-colored mirrors, thinking we see statesmen of yesteryear rather than politicians of today, selfless sacrifice rather than self-serving arrogance.

> " *A bum knee is still a bum knee, and a wrinkle-free corpse is still a corpse."*

The truth is that there never have been enough good leaders. Homes, churches, businesses, nations – all have always needed more and better leaders than society has provided. That shortage of leaders seems strange in our time because we place so much emphasis on training leaders. From the beginning of their school experience, we want our children to be leaders, to excel in academics, athletics, social graces, every measurable category. Business and professional people know the process never ends. Every day's mail brings information about a new seminar, or a new DVD series, or a new this or that purported to improve leadership skills.

Is it possible that we are looking for leadership in all the wrong places?

John W. Gardner, President of the Carnegie Corporation and Secretary of Health, Education, and Welfare in President Lyndon Johnson's cabinet, wrote in 1961, "The society which scorns excellence in plumbing as a humble activity and tolerates shoddiness in philosophy because it is an exalted activity will have neither good plumbing nor good philosophy; neither its pipes nor its theories will hold water."

Gardner had a way with words, but the word we still pursue is Success! We're conditioned to dress for success, to use the right kind of toothpaste, the right perfume or aftershave, drive the right kind of car, drink the right wine, attend the right school, and we'll be "successful!" Though we are not astronauts, we can all have the "right stuff." We can all be trim, athletic, fashionably gray, jut-jawed winners!

We know better, of course. Whoever claims "sixty is the new forty" needs a reality check. A bum knee is still a bum knee, and a wrinkle-free corpse is still a corpse. Even as we read or watch the ads we smile and think, "How gullible do you think I am?" Then we go to the mall or sit down at the computer terminal and, before we know it, our gullibility has been revealed.

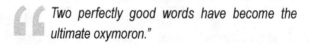

> *Two perfectly good words have become the ultimate oxymoron."*

A father desperately wanted his daughter to attend a prestigious women's college, but he was stymied by the question on the parent's form: "Is your daughter a leader?" His conscience finally won over his ambition and he answered, "In all honesty, no, my daughter is not a leader, but she is an exceptionally good follower." Then he listed some of her accomplishments. Sometime later, his hands trembled as he opened the reply from the Dean of Admissions: "Dear Sir, inasmuch as our incoming class is comprised almost entirely of leaders and few followers, your daughter's application is gratefully accepted."

When we bow to the gods of success and the fame that often accompanies leadership, we need to be reminded that the best kind of leadership (indeed, the only kind of Kingdom leadership) is servant leadership. A cynical society finds it hard to believe that a person can be a "public servant." Two perfectly good words have become the ultimate oxymoron.

> *For even the Son of Man did not come to be served, but to serve, and to give his life as a ransom for many" (Mark 10:45, NIV).*

Long before "Leading from Behind" became a controversial strategy for building international coalitions, Jesus turned conventional wisdom upside down when two followers sought places of prominence:

> *Whoever wants to become great among you ... must be your servant, and whoever wants to be first must be slave of all. For even the Son of Man did not come to be served, ... but to serve, and to give his life as a ransom for many" (Mark 10:44, 45, NIV).*

Can you imagine the embarrassment his followers must have felt when, at the last Passover meal before Jesus' death, his followers were still vying for position when Jesus, their Lord and Master, began to wash their feet (John 13:12-17, NIV). "For whoever exalts himself will be humbled, and whoever humbles himself will be exalted" (Matthew 23:12, ASV). These are puzzling but encouraging words. I once considered taking out a full-page newspaper ad that would say "Need help? Call this number." I thought it was a great idea, but I didn't want to give my number! And I once knew a man whose business card identified him as "A Servant of Christ. How may I serve you?" Do we need to order some more cards?

CHAPTER NINE

Pay it Forward

> *Their meal lasted longer than ours because there was no rushing his feeding."*

The Christmas season in 1996 was bittersweet for our family. Just four days before the holiday, Mary Margaret's mother died at the age of ninety-nine. She had been in a nursing home for several years, and for several months, had hardly been aware of her surroundings. Her life of faith insulated her from any fear of the future. The sadness of our loss was tempered by the joy of her home going.

> *If she asks, just tell her Christmas came early and a follower of Jesus left something for her family."*

All the arrangements for the funeral had been made well in advance. As we traveled to conduct her memorial and attend to her burial, we pulled off the interstate for lunch. After a short wait, the hostess seated us near a mother and three children. The two younger children required little attention, a good thing because the mom was fully occupied with the teenage boy. He was in a special wheelchair, and not able to do anything for himself.

My work with the Muscular Dystrophy Association made me think he had a neuro-muscular disorder. He and his mother had some special bond that let them communicate, and she fed him the bites he wanted, carefully using the napkins to wipe his face and keep food from his clothes. Their meal lasted longer than ours because there was no rushing his feeding.

After I paid our check and was waiting in the entryway, I stopped the perky, cheer-leader type young girl who had served us and asked, "Can you keep a secret?" "Sure!" she said, "what is it?" I explained that I wanted to buy a gift card and have her deliver it to the woman at our neighboring table. "But" I said, "You must wait until we have gone, and you can't identify us in any way. If she asks, just tell her Christmas came early and a follower of Jesus left something for her family." The tears in her eyes were accompanied by her kiss on my cheek.

> *She reached for my hand, and we rode several miles just basking in the glow of being able to help make someone's Christmas a little brighter."*

As we got back on the highway, Mary Margaret asked, "What happened back there while I was in the rest room?" "Nothing," I fibbed. "I know you too well," she said, "and something happened." I told her the story, she reached for my hand, and we rode several miles just basking in the glow of being able to help make someone's Christmas a little brighter. Unspoken was our mutual awareness of how much like Mary Margaret's mother, Florence Hannahs Discher, our small act of service had been.

When Catherine Ryan Hyde's book *Pay It Forward* was published four years later, I was glad somebody had put a label on what we had tried to do. Though the book and movie are modern, the concept may be as old as ancient Greece. Hyde's book, which also became an acclaimed movie by the same name, is the fictional account of seventh-grade student Trevor McKinney who had an unusual Social Studies assignment. He was assigned the task of devising and putting into action a plan to change the world for the better – quite a task for anybody, let alone a seventh grader! The movie featured such stars as Kevin Spacey, Helen Hunt, Angie Dickinson, Jim Caviezel, and Jon Bon Jovi. The book was published in 23 languages, distributed in more than 30 countries, and reissued at least once.

> *At its best, payback is returning a kindness. At its worst, it can be resentful duty, or even harsh retaliation."*

The imaginary Trevor proved equal to the task. His solution was to do something nice for three people, asking them only to "pay it forward" by doing something nice for three others.

We are all too familiar with "paying it backward," so much so that "payback" has become a word with a dictionary definition. At its best, payback is returning a kindness. At its worst, it can be resentful duty, or even harsh retaliation. We've all had the conversations: "They didn't invite us to the reception after their daughter's wedding; why should we....?" "Yeah, they send us a Christmas card every year; guess we'd better...." "We've had them over for dinner twice and they never...."

> *You don't have to join anything or buy anything, just do something nice for somebody."*

Growing out of the book and movie is The *Pay It Forward* Foundation, which has designated Thursday, April 25, 2013, as *Pay It Forward* Day. They hope people will respond by performing

5 million acts of kindness on that day. You don't have to join anything or buy anything, just do something nice for somebody.

I still like to call the server over and say, "Can you keep a secret? Do you see that couple with two small children at the table in the corner? Can you keep a secret and *Pay It Forward*"? – two ways to speak Encouraging Words.

CHAPTER TEN

Catching Flies

> *I thought upgrading to an electric typewriter and a push-button telephone would be easy, but I hadn't counted on inheriting an immovable object."*

She was two years older than my mother. Although they had never met, they shared the conviction that, at age twenty-six, I was much too young to be preaching for the largest congregation in the state. I dared not let them know they were right. She was the long-time church secretary I inherited. Lady was her name – Lady Marie – but it could easily have been her title. She would have been very much at home in a royal court in an earlier century.

> *This letter is harsh and negative, and you'll be sorry if you send it. You catch more flies with honey than with vinegar."*

There wasn't much office equipment in those days – no FAX machines, no photocopiers worth mentioning, no computers, no cell phones. But her manual Smith-Corona typewriter with the misaligned keys (Smith-Corona because they made one in robin-egg blue, her favorite color), and black, rotary dial telephone were inadequate, even for that time. I thought upgrading to an electric typewriter and a push-button telephone would be easy, but I hadn't counted on inheriting an immovable object.

In those days, secretaries knew Gregg shorthand and carried a steno pad wherever they went. As I was dictating a letter one day, I noticed that Lady Marie had stopped writing. Pencil in hand, steno pad in her lap, she just sat there. "Am I going too fast for you?" I asked. "No," she said, "but I don't think you should send this letter. It is harsh and negative, and you'll be sorry if you send it. You catch more flies with honey than with vinegar." "But I'm not catching flies," I protested, "I'm giving this person a piece of my mind and trying to straighten him out!" I think she muttered something about not having any pieces to spare, but I'm sure I heard her say, "You'll just make matters worse, and, besides, you catch more flies with honey than with vinegar."

Determined to make my point, after she left, I pulled out my portable typewriter and began to bang away, writing my own letter, proof-reading as I went. As the inflammatory words appeared on the page, it slowly dawned on me that she was right: the letter should never be sent. I'm not even sure I finished it, but know I never sent it. I could indeed catch more flies with honey than with vinegar.

> *The note was held in place by a unique paperweight – a jar of Orange Blossom Honey."*

But I still wanted better equipment for our office. As equipment salesmen paraded through, explaining the mechanical superiority of their products, Lady Marie was thumbing through their brochures, looking for the color chart. It didn't take long, because most of the companies had adopted the Henry Ford Model T philosophy: "You can have any color you want so long as it's black." Finally, Smith-Corona agreed to paint one of their electric typewriters robin-egg blue and I was on my way. Things were looking good when one of our deacons who was an executive with the telephone company (there was only one in those days) arranged to have his shop spray paint a push-button phone in robin-egg blue.

I bided my time until Lady Marie went on vacation. On the Monday morning she returned to work, on her desk were a beautiful, robin-egg blue electric typewriter, a matching robin-egg blue push-button telephone, and a note from me: "Please forgive me, but I know we both want what's best for this church. I put your old typewriter and phone in the closet. Please try these new ones for thirty days and, if you just don't like them, we'll put your old ones back in service." The note was held in place by a unique paperweight – a jar of Orange Blossom Honey.

> *She and my mother formed a protective wall the newly franchised Miami Dolphins could have used."*

I got to the office early that morning, not knowing what to expect. I heard her come in and waited several minutes for her to come in my office. When she did, her eyes still red, she said simply, "I'm going to try really hard." "Thank you," I said, "I know you will because you love this church." "And I love you," she said, stepping close enough to give me a long-distance hug. I didn't dare tell her I had been shopping for robin-egg blue dictation equipment. From that day forward, she was my second-staunchest defender. She and my mother formed a protective wall the newly franchised Miami Dolphins could have used.

The concept, if not the exact words, is found throughout the Bible.

> *A gentle answer ... turns away wrath, but a harsh word ... stirs up anger" (Proverbs 15:1, NIV).*

> *Kind words ... are like honey – they cheer you up ... and make you feel strong" (Proverbs 16:24, CEV).*

And surely the idea is included in the admonition of Jesus about treating others as we would like to be treated in Matthew 7:12, ASV).

"You can catch more flies with honey than with vinegar" – Encouraging Words I should never forget, but often do.

CHAPTER ELEVEN

Run... Walk... Crawl... Finish!

> *Our tragedies have a way of bringing out the best in us."*

What a week! Two terrorist bombs put a devastating punctuation mark at the finish line of the 116th Boston Marathon, killing three and injuring 264. A fertilizer plant exploded in the small town of West, Texas, killing at least fourteen and injuring 200. Three letters laced with deadly ricin poison were intercepted before they could reach the President, a U. S. senator, and a county judge. Floods in the Midwest may break records that have stood for 70 years. With all those things happening in a single week, is there any possible way to find some encouraging words? In a word, Yes.

> *Personal pain becomes community pain. The mantra for West became 'When everything falls apart, we come together.'"*

Our tragedies have a way of bringing out the best in us. Even with those events crowding everything else out of several news cycles, and almost every word being another hammer blow of despair, encouraging words were found in unlikely places. Who would have thought that a post on a website in Wales could inspire 34,000 runners in the London Marathon, just six days after Boston? Those runners caught the spirit, it spread to thousands more lining the 26.2 mile course, and soon the whole world listened: "Run if you can, walk if you have to, but finish for Boston." No one knows for sure, but it is thought the slogan originated with a contestant on the TV reality show The Biggest Loser. As she finished a twelve-mile run in three hours and one minute, friends noticed that her headband read, "Run, Walk, Crawl, Finish!"

> *Finally finishing way behind the leaders, he was congratulating a fellow runner when the bomb went off."*

West, Texas, a small town of 2,800, was almost destroyed by the explosion registering 2.1 on the Richter scale, a reading usually associated with a small earthquake. In a town the size of West, lots of people are related to one another and everybody knows everybody else. Personal pain becomes community pain. The mantra for West became "When everything falls apart, we come together."

Rob Wheeler hadn't planned to run the marathon this year. But when a friend became ill and handed Rob his number, the man who had not thought of being a hero ran though he had not trained. At mile 16, his knee locked up and he had to rest for a while. At mile 25, he stopped to help a woman runner who had fallen.

> *Let us fix our eyes on Jesus, the author and perfecter of our faith... so that [we] will not grow weary and lose heart (Hebrews 12:2,3, NASB)."*

Finally finishing way behind the leaders, he was congratulating a fellow runner when the bomb went off. Uninjured, but wandering in a daze, he saw a woman leaning over a man and crying, "Somebody help my dad; he's badly hurt!" When he saw the man's leg wounds bleeding profusely, Rob took off his shirt, used it for a bandage and tourniquet, elevated the man's leg, and stayed with him until the medics arrived. Knowing only the man's name was Ron, he tried and finally did find Ron Brassard in the hospital. Rob, 23, and Ron, 51, quickly became like father and son. "Our whole family is planning to attend Rob's May 19 graduation [from Framingham State University]," said Ron, "We're part of each other's life now."

Carlos Arredondo, one of the few men in Boston wearing a cowboy hat, went to the marathon to hand out 200 American flags to honor his sons. Alexander was a 20-year-old Marine killed in Iraq. Younger brother Brian took his own life, leaving a letter about how his brother died. Carlos had given out all the flags but one when the bomb went off. When he saw a man trying to stand and realized both his legs had been blown off, Carlos used his remaining flag and his sweater to fashion tourniquets. He then grabbed a wheelchair and ran as fast as he could to the medical tent, pinching an artery to stop the blood. He said over and over, "My name's Carlos, you're going to be OK, help is on the way." Jeff Bauman did survive, thanks to a grieving, grizzled guy in a cowboy hat.

The Hebrews preacher said it better than I can: "Therefore, since we are surrounded by such a great cloud of witnesses, let us throw off everything that hinders and the sin that so easily entangles, and let us run with perseverance the race marked out for us. Let us fix our eyes on Jesus, the author and perfecter of our faith… so that [we] will not grow weary and lose heart" (Hebrews 12:1-3, NIV).

Run if you can, walk if you have to, crawl if you must, but finish! Encouraging Words!

CHAPTER TWELVE

It Is Finished!

> *With everything before pointing toward him and everything after pointing back to him, Jesus remains the center of our being, and his death and resurrection the central events of human history."*

I smile a bit when I see a date noted as BCE (Before Common Era) or CE (Common Era). From the sixth century until recent times, dates have been noted as BC (Before Christ) or AD (Anno Domini, in the year of our Lord). I smile because changing the notation hasn't changed a thing. The year 2013 CE is exactly the same as the year 2013 AD. With everything before pointing toward him and everything after pointing back to him, Jesus remains the center of our being, and his death and resurrection the central events of human history.

> *There's a line that's been drawn thru the ages, on that line stands the old rugged cross."*

My friend preached at one of the largest churches in America. With 16,000 on the membership roll, 7,000 seats in the worship center, and multiple services on Saturday night and Sunday, he routinely preached to more than 15,000 each week. Special programs on the days around Christmas and Easter reached 50,000 people. Those special services always exalted God and inspired Mary Margaret and me.

At one Easter season, the choir began a song I had never heard. Straining to catch the words I later learned had been written by Bill and Gloria Gaither, I was soon caught up in the majestic message:

There's a line that's been drawn thru the ages, on that line stands the old rugged cross.

On that cross a battle is raging, for the gain of man's soul or his loss.

The next three verses described the conflict between the "devils of hell" and the "angels of glory," the earthquake and the darkening of the sun. Then verse five heralded the triumph, the victory Jesus won:

Then I heard that the King of the Ages had fought all the battles for me:

And the vict'ry was mine for the claiming, and now, praise His name, I am free.

> 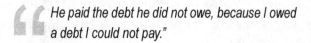 He paid the debt he did not owe, because I owed a debt I could not pay."

Then, for the fifth time, the Refrain thundered the proclamation that brought everyone in the large audience to their feet, most of us wiping away tears at the wonder of it all:

It is finished! The battle is over, It is finished! There'll be no more war.

It is finished! The end of the conflict, It is finished, and Jesus is Lord!

The theme of the song comes straight from the cross. When Jesus complained of thirst, some people around the cross wet a sponge with wine vinegar and held it to his lips.

> *When he had received the drink, Jesus said, 'It is finished.' With that, he bowed his head ... and gave up his spirit" (John 19:30, NLT).*

Bible commentators are not agreed on the meaning of this simple sentence, but my own feeling is that he was declaring done the work he had come to do. "He paid the debt he did not owe, because I owed a debt I could not pay."

As we encourage people to do good works, they sometimes get the idea that good works will purchase their salvation. Not so. "Jesus paid it all; all to him I owe. Sin had left its crimson stain; he washed it white as snow." I will love the Lord my God with all my heart and with all my soul and with all my mind in gratitude for all that is embodied in those Encouraging Words, It Is Finished!

"We celebrate in worship on the Lord's day to ensure that the central event of our faith will never be forgotten.

Its date related to both the lunar phases and the Jewish Passover, Easter has an established place in the calendar. That long-ago day when visitors to the garden found the tomb empty would later be called the Lord's Day, Sunday, and Easter Sunday; the Bible simply calls it "the first day of the week" (John 20:1, NIV). We celebrate in worship on that day to ensure that the central event of our faith will never be forgotten.

After Satan had failed to ensnare Jesus with his usual temptations (Matthew 4:1-11 NIV), he had one other weapon. With Jesus dead, the Father would have no one else to save his creation, or to save me. But Jesus had the power over death, for both himself and us. His work on earth finished, he went to the grave. And then, on that glorious Easter Sunday, "Up from the grave he arose! Hallelujah! Christ arose."

> *It is because of him that you are in Christ Jesus, who has become for us wisdom from God – that is, our righteousness, holiness and redemption" (1 Corinthians 1:30, NIV).*

CHAPTER THIRTEEN

He Is Risen Indeed!

> *Eastern Orthodox, Armenian, Roman Catholic, Greek Orthodox. Coptic, Ethiopian, and Syrian groups contend for control and sometimes resort to physical violence to protect their turf."*

The Garden Tomb is one of the most incredible – in both senses of the word – places in all Jerusalem. Incredible because there isn't any evidence that the crucified Jesus was buried and raised from the dead in that place. And, incredible because it is so extraordinary, so unusual, that it can't be ignored. These days, if you hear something described as UNN-BEE-LEEV-able (with the cadence and emphasis just so) you know that the unbelievable is both believable and compelling. The Garden Tomb is both unbelievable and UNN-BEE-LEEV-able.

As early as the second century, Christians identified the site where the Church of the Holy Sepulcher now stands as possibly the place where Jesus was crucified and buried. Eusebius says that the Emperor Hadrian had the site filled with earth and a temple to Aphrodite constructed on the site. Emperor Constantine, having converted to Christianity, ordered that temple destroyed, the fill dirt removed, and the site restored to its original state.

> *Volunteer guides, most from the United Kingdom, remind visitors over and over that the focus is on the story, not the place."*

Assisting in that work was his mother, Helena, whom he had charged with identifying sites where significant Christian events had occurred and building churches over many of them. Helena purportedly found "proof" of the crucifixion and burial site with the discovery of the "True Cross." A church built on the site in 326 was destroyed by Muslims in 1009, with reconstruction beginning a few years later. The history of the church it housed has been stormy. Even now, Eastern Orthodox, Armenian, Roman Catholic, Greek Orthodox. Coptic, Ethiopian, and Syrian groups contend for control and sometimes resort to physical violence to protect their turf.

Alongside this internal controversy has been external doubt that the Church of the Holy Sepulcher is the real location of Jesus' burial and resurrection. Among the doubters was British General Charles George Gordon who, looking out from a friend's house one day, saw an outcropping of rock in the shape of a skull. He learned that, as early as 1842 a German theologian had seen the same rock cliff and called it "skull hill." It would eventually be known as "Gordon's Calvary" and the "Garden Tomb."

His interest sharpened, in 1867 Gordon discovered a near-by tomb, then a wine press, and other indications that the site had once been a vineyard or garden. Underneath the site there is still a huge cistern, more than fifty feet deep, and large enough to hold approximately 250,000 gallons of water, essential to growing plants in the hot, dry Jerusalem climate. After complicated negotiations, the Garden Tomb Association was formed and purchased the site in 1894. Still operated as a ministry of churches in the United Kingdom, the Garden Tomb Association makes no charge for admission or guides and will even provide communion service on request.

> *Pilgrims are so eager to see the tomb they pass right by the message on the door: HE IS NOT HERE – FOR HE IS RISEN."*

Walk with me from a crowded city street, down a narrow alley, approximately the length of a football field through an obstacle course of vendors and beggars. Passing through the gate at the end of the alley, we step into another world. Flowers are everywhere, birds are singing, everything is lush and green. Within a matter of feet, city noises are forgotten, and even the diesel smells from the adjacent bus station seem to disappear. Down winding pathways, past quiet pools of water, strategically placed benches for prayer or meditation, signs with scripture verses, we come to a rock cliff with a cave-like opening and a tomb inside. Is it? Could it be?

The Garden Tomb Association makes no claim for authenticity, their literature saying simply "where Jesus died is of little importance compared with why." Volunteer guides, most from the United Kingdom, remind visitors over and over that the focus is on the story, not the place. Most visitors to the Garden Tomb never see the real message, though it is in plain sight. The rolling stone that once sealed the entrance to the tomb is no longer there. In its place is a heavy wooden door that is opened back against the wall. Pilgrims are so eager to see the tomb they pass right by the message on the door: HE IS NOT HERE – FOR HE IS RISEN.

> *But Christ has indeed... been raised from the dead, the first fruits of those who have fallen asleep. For since death came through a man, the resurrection of the dead comes also through a man. For as in Adam all die, so ...in Christ all will be made alive"* (1 Corinthians 15:20-22, NIV).

For centuries it has been customary for Christians to meet with an exchange of greetings: "He Is Risen!" "He Is Risen Indeed!" Encouraging Words! Encouraging Words Indeed!

CHAPTER FOURTEEN

Red to Honor, White to Remember

> *As if to hide the worst features of an industrial plant, DuPont planted thousands of rambling rose bushes along the several hundred feet of chain link fence fronting the property."*

Growing up in a family with no sisters and only one brother, I resented and even hated some of the chores my mother assigned me – dusting furniture, washing dishes, cleaning windows – "girlie work!" But there was one chore I neither hated nor resented, maybe because I only did it once a year, but mainly because I sensed that it had special meaning.

> *I would search for the choicest rosebuds, a red one for me, a smaller red one for my brother because he was younger, and white ones for my mom and dad."*

Our small town was owned – literally – by the DuPont Company. DuPont owned the houses and rented them to employees. The company named the schools, owned the utility services, provided police and fire protection, and reminded us of its paternalistic presence daily. Old Hickory was the quintessential company town. Of course, the power plant belched black smoke and noxious fumes – practices common in those days. Hanging over us like a cloud was the ever-present rotten-egg smell from the chemical plant. When visitors asked how we could stand it, we smiled and said it smelled like bread and butter.

As if to hide the worst features of an industrial plant, DuPont planted thousands of rambling rose bushes along the several hundred feet of chain link fence fronting the property. The flowers bloomed continuously for about ten months of the year, their beauty masking the reality inside.

Those rose bushes have everything to do with the once-a-year chore I loved. Early on a Sunday morning each May, I would run or ride my bike to that fence. There I would search for the choicest rosebuds, a red one for me, a smaller red one for my brother because he was younger, and white ones for my mom and dad. Taking out my pocketknife (every boy carried one in those days, blades honed to razor sharpness so we could whittle the thinnest shavings), I would carefully cut the chosen buds and take them home. There we would pin them to our clothes and be ready for church on Mother's Day.

> *We still have those old color slides of our family ready for church, four little stair-step kids and mom and dad, all with red flowers on Mother's Day, boutonnieres for the boys, corsages for the girls."*

When I tell people about that annual chore, and explain that a red flower meant your mother was living and a white one meant she was dead, they often get a puzzled look as if they've never heard the story. For our family, it's a tradition I hope we never lose. After I left home and Mary Margaret and I married and our children came, the tradition continued. We still have those old color slides of our family ready for church, four little stair-step kids and mom and dad, all with red flowers on Mother's Day, boutonnieres for the boys, corsages for the girls. When we lived hundreds of miles away and I could no longer snitch rosebuds from the fence at The Plant, I would make my annual phone call to the Friendly Flower Shop and order white flowers for my mother delivered to 81 Jones Circle.

We knew the time was coming, but we were still unprepared. I remember the stunned realization as I ordered our Mother's Day flowers in 1997. "A red rose for me," I told the Kroger flower-shop lady, "and a red corsage…no, you'd better make that white, for my wife." Mary Margaret's mother had died the previous December, and for the first time ever her Mother's Day corsage would be white. And I vividly remember my own emotions four Mother's Days later when, for the first time in my life, I wore white on Mother's Day.

Anna Jarvis began the practice that became our American tradition when she honored her own deceased mother with a special day of remembrance at a Methodist Church in Grafton, West Virginia in 1908. By 1914 she had campaigned so successfully that President Woodrow Wilson signed into law the proclamation passed by both houses of Congress making Mother's Day a national holiday. Both Jarvis and the President insisted that the spelling be singular possessive – Mother's Day – to encourage a personal rather than generic observance.

Next Mother's Day, I will wear my white flower, and I will know why my mother always had a tear in her eye as she pinned on the white bud I so carefully selected. If you can still wear red, thank God! If you must wear white, thank God! Red to honor… white to remember…Encouraging Words!

For you know that it was not with perishable things such as silver or gold that you were redeemed from the empty way of life handed down to you from your ancestors, but with the precious blood of Christ, a lamb without blemish or defect" (1 Peter 1:18,19, NIV).

CHAPTER FIFTEEN

Broken Hearts and Living Spirits

> It was almost unbelievable that the lead singer was Francine Wheeler, who somehow found the strength to sing just 58 days after her son's murder."

I don't remember when I first noticed Bill Moyers. It may have been in 1962 when he became Deputy Director of the Peace Corps, or, more likely, in 1965 when he became Press Secretary for President Lyndon B. Johnson. We had a few things in common, such as our age (he's a year younger) and our vocation (he was a young preacher in Baptist churches and I in Churches of Christ). As I followed his journalistic career and read his books, I was impressed by his integrity and in-depth reporting. His Friday night Moyers and Company program on public television was must-see TV at our house.

> A nation that refuses to rise up and say, 'Never again' has lost its moral compass."

One Friday night, the program opened as usual with Moyers' face filling the screen, and his customary "Welcome!" greeting. Then the camera pulled back to show the two people across the desk. One was a pretty, young, dark-haired woman, smiling through tear-filled eyes. The other was a man, balding, smiling, though his eyes were also teary. Seventy-four-year-old Peter Yarrow is known to my generation as part of the Peter Paul and Mary trio. Francine Wheeler was not widely known until December 14, 2012 when her son Benjamin was one of twenty children shot to death by a deranged gunman at Sandy Hook Elementary School in Connecticut.

As Moyers and his guests relived the painful story, they talked about the concert held on February 10, 2013 to honor the Sandy Hook victims and support their families. A video clip from the concert showed Peter Yarrow with his guitar, a small band, and some vocalists. It was almost unbelievable that the lead singer was Francine Wheeler, who somehow found the strength to sing just 58 days after her son's murder. The lump in my throat refused to move when her clear, soprano voice sang, "How many roads must a man walk down...."

I had heard those haunting words on August 28, 1963. On that day it was the late Mary Travers, with Peter Yarrow and Paul Stookey who sang to set the stage for Dr. Martin Luther King's culture-changing "I Have a Dream" speech delivered to a crowd of 250,000 gathered at the National Mall in Washington.

> *Legislators who voted against the gun-violence bill... because 'it didn't go far enough' have a moral obligation to pass a bill that does go far enough."*

How many times must the cannonballs fly before they are forever banned?

How many times can a man turn his head and pretend that he just doesn't see?

How many deaths will it take till he knows that too many people have died?

The same response followed each question: "The answer, my friend, is blowing in the wind; the answer is blowing in the wind."

Despite the efforts of local courts, school boards, governors, and, yes, even churches, to perpetuate racial segregation, it was in its death throes. Stopping Dr. King's dream was as impossible as stopping a hurricane. The assassin's bullet killed him, but it could not kill his dream. There was an unstoppable pressure for change; the answer was blowing in the wind.

> Asked how he was dealing with his grief, [David Wheeler] answered with two sentences that are stamped on my heart: 'There is no way out of my grief, but there is a way through it.... My heart is broken; my spirit is not.'"

Encouraging Words is about moral, not political issues. The murder of twenty children is a moral issue. And a nation that refuses to rise up and say, "Never again" has lost its moral compass. Legislators who voted against the gun-violence bill co-sponsored by courageous Republican Senator Pat Toomey and equally courageous Democratic Senator Joe Manchin because "it didn't go far enough" have a moral obligation to pass a bill that does go far enough. Voting no and doing nothing is not the solution. There is an innate goodness in Americans that will not tolerate forever the violence that robs children of their most fundamental right – the right to life. The change that is blowing in the wind may not come soon, but it will come because it cannot be stopped.

David Wheeler joined his wife on Moyers' show just as he had joined her onstage in Newtown. Asked how he was dealing with his grief, he answered with two sentences that are stamped on my heart: "There is no way out of my grief, but there is a way through it….My heart is broken; my spirit is not." In the darkest of hours, these are Encouraging Words.

CHAPTER SIXTEEN

Blessed Are the Dead Who Die in the Lord

> It didn't take long for me to see in Keith someone who was not only good enough for Bryn, but ideal for Bryn."

I don't remember the first time I met Keith Kreidel, but I'm quite sure I wasn't very nice to him. As they neared dating age, I told both of our daughters that I would probably not be nice to anyone they dated seriously because there was nobody good enough for them. With that prejudice firmly in place, I met Keith – Keith with that almost Afro head of hair, Keith who was always smiling and laughing, Keith who couldn't be still, always stretching, exercising, jumping, running, doing his ballet imitations. Didn't the man have a serious bone in his body?

> Mary Margaret said quietly, 'We didn't raise our children to live next door.'"

As a matter of fact, he did. Beneath that façade was a serious person, a deep thinker, a committed Christian, a man who had never gotten his love for Brazil out of his system. It didn't take long for me to see in Keith someone who was not only good enough for Bryn, but ideal for Bryn.

Long distance phone calls were not nearly as common in the 70s and 80s as they are now, so we tend to remember them better. I remember the afternoon Bryn called me at work and said, "You have probably figured out by now that Keith and I are going to get married, but I don't think you could know that we are planning to be missionaries in Brazil. I really need you to help me with Mom." "Help you with Mom?" I shouted, "Who's going to help you with me?"

Sometime later we attended a weekend retreat for parents of people on the Brazil Mission Team. I heard about the session for mothers that Mary Margaret attended, sitting patiently while some mothers wept and bemoaned the fact that their children were going so far away. When it came her turn, Mary Margaret said quietly, "We didn't raise our children to live next door." We had tried to give our two boys and two girls the roots of a solid grounding in Scripture, a solid sense of values, roots that could withstand any challenge, and wings to free them for self-expression and adventure, even beyond the safe haven that was home. Walter and Mary Nelle also had two boys and two girls they raised with similar roots and wings.

For a part of their college careers, Bryn, Jim, and Janet were all at Abilene Christian University at the same time. It was during that time that Keith called me one night, his nervousness so obvious even over the long-distance line that I could almost feel his sweaty palms. After considerable stuttering and stammering, he finally managed to say, "I'm calling to say that I would like to marry your daughter!" When I blurted out, "Which one?" that didn't do a thing to calm his nerves. That call became an important part of our family lore. I quickly assured Keith that we would be honored to have him for our son-in-law, and on December 21, 1979, Walter and I jointly officiated, joining our children in marriage that would end only in death.

> *On most Sundays, Keith could probably have preached a better sermon than he heard."*

I was always proud to introduce Keith as my son-in-law, though Mary Margaret and I always thought of him as a son. We had two sons, but we could certainly make room in our hearts for another one. He was Keith and I was Dad. It wasn't unusual for him to call and say, "I'm reading this book I think you'd like, and when I finish, I'll send it to you." Or, he might call and say, "I found this shower soap I really like at World Market; I'll send you a couple of bars."

On most Sundays, Keith could probably have preached a better sermon than he heard. He could have been a great teacher of adult classes and could have inspired a gym full of teenagers. But he chose to work in the nursery, to care for the babies who needed fresh diapers, or a bottle, or to be rocked, or sung to. He was a great husband and father, and would have been the greatest, most indulgent granddad ever.

> *Rooted and grounded in our faith, we look to the God of all comfort who has promised, 'I will never leave you nor forsake you'" (Joshua 1:5, KJV).*

Mary Margaret and I have been so sad this week, feeling so deeply the pain that Bryn, Emmy and Nick, Joe and Melissa, Annie, Jesse, and Abby are feeling even more deeply. Abraham

Lincoln said, "The Almighty has his own purposes." Like Job of old, I would really like to know what those purposes are. Rooted and grounded in our faith, we look to the God of all comfort who has promised,

> " *I will never... leave you ...nor forsake you" (Joshua 1:5, KJV).*

> " *Blessed are the dead... who die in the Lord.... they will rest from their labor, ...for their deeds will follow them" (Revelation 14:13, NIV).*

Although blurred by our tears, those are Encouraging Words.

CHAPTER SEVENTEEN

Stop by the Lobby and See my Underwear

> Rochester College Associates and its predecessor organization founded by Bette Huckaby, has raised over $4 million."

Lovine Beth Johnson was a small-town girl from Ashby, Minnesota, and William Overton Huckaby, Jr. was a small-town boy from Columbia, Tennessee. In 1943, Bette wanted to be part of the action in World War II, so she became a WAC, enlisting in the Women's Army Corps. Bill was also a soldier, and these two young adults, in what they would later describe as an act of providence, were assigned to work in the same office in Tampa, Florida. There the soldier and the WAC fell in love and married following a whirlwind courtship lasting only a few weeks. The courtship was brief, but the marriage was enduring, lasting forty-two years, ended by Bill's untimely death.

> If the preacher paused too long, Bette might just offer a few words to help him fill the void. Bette

> thought some songs could not be sung appropriately sitting down, so, when one of those songs began, she stood up."

Mary Margaret and I first met Bette and Bill Huckaby in 1959 when I was a young preacher at the Northwest Church of Christ in Detroit, and they were active members of a different congregation.

When people in the Detroit area began talking about establishing the Christian college that began as North Central Christian College, became Michigan Christian, and is now Rochester University, Bette thought women ought to get involved. She enlisted some friends to help, had Bill construct a portable display, and began selling pies and cakes to support the fledgling school. Rochester College Associates and its predecessor organization founded by Bette Huckaby, has raised over $4 million.

When the Woodmont Hills church in Nashville outgrew its parking lot, we arranged to use part of a lot at a neighbor church. We then asked for volunteers to park down the hill, across the busy street, and make room for others in our own parking lot. No one was surprised to see a little old lady named Bette park as far away as possible, cross the street and trudge up the hill.

Bette made it her personal mission to speak to as many people as possible and make as many friends as possible. She always sat about three rows from the front, and if the preacher paused too long, Bette might just offer a few words to help him fill the void. Bette thought some songs could not be sung properly sitting down, so, when one of those songs began, she stood up. If nobody stood with her, that did not bother her a bit.

> " Bette would put up a table in the church lobby, cover it with red, white, and blue bunting, and display her wartime memorabilia, including her WAC

> *uniform, complete down to the khaki underwear. She shocked many an unsuspecting visitor by saying, 'Be sure to stop by the lobby and see my underwear!'*

Bette never wavered in her love for God and country. She was a patriot, through and through. On Memorial Day weekend, Bette would put up a table in the church lobby, cover it with red, white, and blue bunting, and display her wartime memorabilia, including her WAC uniform, complete down to the khaki underwear. She shocked many an unsuspecting visitor by saying, "Be sure to stop by the lobby and see my underwear!" The words never before heard in church caused many to stop and think rather than just walk on by.

Originally called Decoration Day, the day to honor Americans who died in war became known as Memorial Day. From the time of the Revolutionary War until now, approximately 1.3 million Americans have died in war, almost half of them in the Civil War. Memorial Day does not promote war or justify war; it honors the memory of those who have served our country valiantly.

> ❝ *I have fought the good fight, I have finished the race, I have kept the faith. Now there is in store for me the crown of righteousness, which the Lord, the righteous Judge, will award to me on that day – and not only to me, but also ...to all who have longed for his appearing" (2 Timothy 4:7,8, NIV).*

I was visiting Bette in the hospital when she learned she had pancreatic cancer so advanced that no treatment was recommended. Bette took in stride the news that would crush most of us. "I have always known I was going to die," she said, "now I know what is going to kill me and approximately when."

After a few days of palliative care, Bette was moved to a hospice facility where she lived just one hour.

On February 26, 2010, Bette's funeral was conducted as she had planned it. As I looked through her well-worn Bible, the verses she had underlined were mostly about peace and joy – characteristics of Bette's life. "I have fought the good fight, I have finished the race, I have kept the faith. Now there is in store for me the crown of righteousness, which the Lord, the righteous Judge, will award to me on that day – and not only to me, but also to all who have longed for his appearing." Encouraging Words from 2 Timothy 4:7, 8, NIV.

CHAPTER EIGHTEEN

It Is Well with my Soul

> *The steamship Ville du Havre on which they sailed collided with another ship on November 2, 1873 and sank in just twelve minutes, claiming the lives of 226 people, including the four Spafford daughters."*

Horatio G. Spafford is hardly a household name, even to regular church goers who have seen his name hundreds of times. Spafford was a Chicago lawyer and real estate investor who made a fortune in downtown Chicago real estate in the years following the Civil War. But he lost everything in the Great Chicago Fire of 1871. Thinking God must have more in mind for them than just rebuilding his fortune, Spafford and his wife, Anna, became ardent supporters of Dwight L. Moody's ministry. In 1873, they decided to take their four young daughters and go to England where they would assist Moody in an evangelistic crusade.

> *Jerusalem is where my Lord lived, suffered and conquered and I wish to learn how to live, suffer and especially to conquer."*

Due to some unforeseen circumstances, Mrs. Spafford and the girls went ahead of Horatio. The steamship Ville du Havre on which they sailed collided with another ship on November 2, 1873 and sank in just twelve minutes, claiming the lives of 226 people, including the four Spafford daughters. Anna Spafford, after being rescued and taken to Wales, sent a cablegram beginning with two ominous words: "Saved alone." One can only imagine the heartache and despair Horatio felt, but it was in the cauldron of this loss that Horatio G. Spafford wrote the beloved hymn *It Is Well with My Soul*.

As they tried to recover from their loss and rebuild their lives, Horatio and Anna had two more children, a son who died of scarlet fever at the age of three, and a daughter who lived to be ninety.

> Bertha, the remaining Spafford daughter, explained that her parents never started a church and never preached a sermon. They just did all the good they could, they helped the poor develop cottage industries and farms, ministering to Arabs and Jews alike."

In 1881, the Spafford family decided to move to Jerusalem, where they spent their remaining years. Horatio explained: "Jerusalem is where my Lord lived, suffered and conquered and I wish to learn how to live, suffer and especially to conquer."

Bertha, the remaining Spafford daughter, explained that her parents never started a church and never preached a sermon. They just did all the good they could, they helped the poor develop cottage industries and farms, ministering to Arabs and Jews alike.

> The famous hotel built around their original residence is known as The American Colony Hotel and is a favorite East Jerusalem place for foreign journalists and diplomats."

They purchased a pasha's palace which became their home and base of operations, and a hospital providing care for injured soldiers on all sides during World War I. A clinic they established to serve young mothers and their babies is still operating more than a hundred years later just inside Herod's Gate in the Old City.

The Spaffords rejected the claim of some church friends that the deaths of their children were divine punishment for sin. Often criticized and even opposed by American consuls for their unconventional religious practices, the Spaffords continued their mission undeterred, gladly accepting "The Overcomers" as a name some gave their movement.

The grand house they purchased and converted into a hospital was converted again into one of the most famous hotels in the world. Local residents referred to the Spaffords as "the Americans," and to their base of operations as "the American colony." The famous hotel built around their original residence is known as The American Colony Hotel and is a favorite East Jerusalem place for foreign journalists and diplomats. During the Second Intifada or uprising in the early years of this century, I once counted seventy vehicles with "foreign press" credentials in the American Colony parking lot. For more than a hundred years, this five-star luxury hotel has been a zone of neutrality in the Arab-Jewish conflict.

> *In a side lobby, just left of the main entrance, is a pictorial history of the Spafford family, with pictures and artifacts showing the family's ministry."*

My friend Joseph Shulam who, with his wife Marcia, lives in Jerusalem and makes it the center from which he preaches all over the world, showed me a special feature of the American Colony which I have shared with hundreds of pilgrims. In a side lobby, just left of the main entrance, is a pictorial history of the Spafford family, with pictures and artifacts showing the family's ministry. Included is a framed sheet of stationery from the Brevoort House Hotel in Chicago on which Horatio G. Spafford wrote these now-famous lines set to music by Phillip P. Bliss in 1876:

> *When peace like a river attendeth my way,*
> *When sorrows like sea billows roll;*
> *Whatever my lot, Thou hast taught me to say,*
> *It is well, it is well with my soul.*

CHAPTER NINETEEN

Well, I Love You Too!

> "I'm an elder in your church, and I love you too much to watch your marriage break up without trying to help. Could I pray with you?"

I was standing in a church lobby when a man I didn't know exclaimed, "You've got to be kin to Paul Morrison because you look just like him!" I replied, "Thank you for the compliment. I had the privilege of being his son, but how did you know my dad?"

> "Daddy died twenty-one years ago; leaving a legacy I'm still trying to claim – a shepherd's heart and a pastor's care."

By this time, his wife had joined him. They told me their names and stood, misty-eyed, with arms around one another, as they told their story: "Fifteen years ago, we were having marital problems and were headed for divorce. Your daddy came out to our house, sat in our living room, and said, 'I'm not a marriage counselor, and I don't know anything about your problems. But I'm an elder in your church, and I love you too much to watch your marriage break up without trying to help. Could I pray with you?' Your daddy prayed a beautiful prayer, and as he was leaving, said, 'There was obviously something that drew you together and caused you to love each other. You had something wonderful and special, and I just hope you will try to find it again before you let your marriage die.' When your daddy left, we just looked at each other, remembering that we did have something special, and here we are, thanks to your daddy!"

> *She was 43 years old before she heard her father say the words she had craved so long: 'I love you.'*

Daddy died twenty-one years ago; leaving a legacy I'm still trying to claim – a shepherd's heart and a pastor's care. On Father's Day, in the year he would have been 107, I cherish his memory.

In the county adjacent to the one where my dad grew up on a tobacco farm, a girl named Patricia Head also grew up on a tobacco farm. She was 43 years old before she heard her father say the words she had craved so long: "I love you." Yet there were glimpses of an unspoken love. When Patricia reported that their school district would no longer have girls' basketball, Richard Head said, "Well, we'll just move." And he moved the family to a district where Patricia could play.

And play she did, so successfully that, at age twenty-two, she became head coach of the University of Tennessee team that became the world-famous Lady Vols. Married, she became known as Pat Summitt and picked up a few honors along the way – 1,098 wins, most in NCAA history by any coach, man or woman; eight national championships; a silver medal as an Olympic player, and a gold one as a coach – the list goes on. As Alzheimer's began robbing her of the ability to function at her customary high level, she reluctantly retired after coaching for 38 years.

> **As Michael rose to leave, he said, 'I just want to tell you I love you.' The President cocked his head in that familiar way and said, 'Well, I love you too!'"**

I accepted the invitation to attend a fund-raising dinner only because it came from my best friends. I didn't have the heart to tell them that the guest speaker, Michael Reagan, was not one of my favorites. To my surprise, I was soon caught up in the challenging things he was saying about family dynamics.

I was particularly interested in his description of the long-standing estrangement between him and his father, former President Ronald Reagan. He told how he realized that somebody had to take the first step toward reconciliation, and that he should be that somebody. Michael was ushered into the Oval Office as if he were there for an ordinary business appointment. The two men spent a few minutes making small talk. Finally, as Michael rose to leave, he said, "I just want to tell you I love you." The President cocked his head in that familiar way and said, "Well, I love you too!" Then the two men held out their arms and embraced each other in a great bear hug. Michael said that every time he saw his father after that, they would hold out their arms and repeat that hug.

The last time Michael Reagan saw his father alive, he and his wife had gone to the home where the former president was in the last stages of Alzheimer's. On that day he was so bad he couldn't get out of bed, and their visit with him was little more than sticking their heads in his bedroom door. After a brief visit with Nancy, she walked them to the door. As Michael opened the car door for his wife, she said, "Michael! Look!" In the doorway where Nancy had been was his father, in his pajamas, somehow standing with his arms outstretched. What a Father's Day memory!

Does somebody in your family need to take that first step? Could that SOMEBODY be You?

For he has rescued us from the dominion of darkness and brought us into the kingdom of the Son he loves, in whom we have redemption, the forgiveness of sins" (Colossians 1:13,14, NIV).

CHAPTER TWENTY

I Don't Even Buy Green Bananas!

> "Predictions are difficult, especially about the future."

1962 was not exactly a banner year for Decca Music. After auditioning two groups, Decca signed one and decided not to sign the other. The one they signed? Brian Poole and the Tremeloes. You remember them, don't you? And the group they turned down? Four guys called The Beatles. Remember them? A Decca executive explained to Brian Epstein, manager of The Beatles, "We don't like your boys' sound. Groups are out; four-piece groups with guitars particularly are finished." Really? Just two years later, The Beatles made their American debut on The Ed Sullivan Show on CBS, and the rest is history.

> "Why predict things all the way to the year 3797 if the world is going to end earlier?"

Maybe Yogi Berra, my second favorite philosopher right after Charlie Brown, was right after all. "Predictions are difficult, especially about the future."

Futurists have always had a hard time, at least as far back as Nostradamus. The 16th century seer and astrologer wrote The Prophecies in such riddles that deciphering his predictions is as hard as determining whether they proved true. Like a lot of others who pretend to know the future, Nostradamus predicted the end of the world in 1994, or maybe 1998, or 2000, or 2012.

Why predict things all the way to the year 3797 if the world is going to end earlier? His cult following of true believers claim he predicted everything from the atomic bomb to the assassinations of John F. and Robert F. Kennedy to Hurricane Katrina to the death of Princess Diana to whatever. Of course, these interpretations by his followers overlook all the times he was wrong.

But he's not the only one. In 1898, New York City hosted the first international urban planning conference, prompted in part by the prediction that by 1930, horse manure in the city would rise to the third-story windows. As Forrest Gump might say, "I believe that's all I'm going to say about that!"

A year later, in 1899, Charles H. Duell, Commissioner of the United States Patent Office, claimed that "Everything that can be invented has been invented."

Thomas Watson, Chairman of IBM, would hardly have agreed with Duell but he was equally wrong when he said in 1943, "I think there is a world market for maybe five computers." And as recently as 1977, Ken Olsen, founder of Digital Equipment Corporation said, "There is no reason anyone would want a computer in their home."

 Predictors of the future have failed most often when trying to predict the end of the world."

Even people as tech savvy as Steve Ballmer, the CEO of Microsoft, was completely wrong when he said in 2007, "There's no chance that the iPhone is going to get any significant market share. No chance." And Time magazine, in a special issue about the future, predicted that on-line shopping would fail because "women like to get out of the house, like to handle the merchandise, like to be able to change their minds." In 2012 on-line shopping produced a trillion (yes, trillion) dollars in sales, and Amazon alone generated $15.7 billion in just the second quarter of 2013.

Predictors of the future have failed most often when trying to predict the end of the world. Michael Stifel, a mathematician, said Judgment Day would begin at 8:00 a.m. on October 19, 1533. Puritan minister Cotton Mather said 1697 was the year, but he revised the date twice. William Miller was sure March 21, 1844 was the time. Herbert W. Armstrong picked 1936 and revised it three times. Televangelist and would-be president Pat Robertson picked 1982, and psychic Edgar Cayce predicted 2000 would be our last year.

A guy like me, so dubious about the future that I don't even buy green bananas, is not going to get caught up in the uncertainty of predicting future events, but will concentrate on getting ready for an event that is as certain as its timing is uncertain.

Not even Jesus would predict the date the world will end.

> *No one knows... about that day or hour, not even the angels in heaven, nor the Son, but only the Father.... Therefore, keep watch, ...because you do not know on what day your Lord will come" (Matthew 24:36, 42, NIV).*

There's a great day coming by and by! Great when we are safe in the arms of Jesus, ready for that day to come.

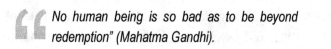 *No human being is so bad as to be beyond redemption" (Mahatma Gandhi).*

CHAPTER TWENTY-ONE

He's with Me

> "A friend of Presidents John F. Kennedy and Lyndon B. Johnson, Billie Sol's appeared to be the ultimate success story."

I don't remember the month or the day, but it was sometime in 1959 when I met Billie Sol Estes. That was the only time I ever met him, and I think the only time I ever saw him. I was a 26-year-old preacher in Detroit, Michigan and he was a 34-year-old, flamboyant Texas businessman, already a high-flying multi-millionaire.

In 1953, the United States Junior Chamber of Commerce had named him one of the ten Outstanding Young Men of America. In 1962, he was on the cover of "Time" magazine.

A friend of Presidents John F. Kennedy and Lyndon B. Johnson, Billie Sol's appeared to be the ultimate success story.

> "It was harder to keep up with Floyd, though I knew that he continued to preach and write, was active in the Civil Rights movement...."

That illusion was quickly shattered in 1963 when he was convicted of fraud and sentenced to spend 24 years in prison. He won parole in 1971 but was convicted of additional fraud and tax evasion charges in 1979, serving another four years in prison.

On the day we met, we were in the Detroit suburb of Rochester, Michigan on the newly acquired campus of a new Christian school that would eventually become Rochester University. Billie Sol was there to consult with our small group about fund raising for the new school. Traveling with Billie Sol was a young black preacher, just 19 years old, being supported by Billie Sol because he thought Floyd Rose showed a lot of promise.

As the years went by, it was easy to keep up with Billie Sol because he was in the news frequently. It was harder to keep up with Floyd, though I knew that he continued to preach and write, was active in the Civil Rights movement, was President of the NAACP chapter in Toledo, Ohio, and Director of Human Relations for the Toledo public schools for a number of years. He retired and moved back home to Valdosta, Georgia where he is the Senior Servant at the Serenity Church he established in 2009.

Some 50 years after our first meeting, my friend Floyd told me how Billie Sol had influenced his life. He was just 11 years old, traveling with the legendary Marshall Keeble as one of "Keeble's Boys" when the group visited in Pecos, Texas, Billie Sol's hometown. Estes saw so much promise in Floyd Rose that he paid for his education at Nashville Christian Institute and Southwestern Christian College, both schools training young black people.

> *Over and over, in fancy restaurants and white-only hotels, Floyd heard those familiar words, 'He's with me.'"*

When Floyd was just 12 years old, Billie Sol wanted him to be the first to spend a night in the guest house he built adjacent to his own home, and where senators, congressmen, and other special friends would later stay. The next morning saw the beginning of a series of events Billie Sol would control with a single sentence uttered again and again. When Floyd ran to get in a chauffeur-driven limousine, the driver challenged, "Hey boy, where do you think you're going?" Billie Sol said simply, "He's with me."

They drove to an airstrip where one of Billie Sol's two airplanes was waiting, and again Floyd was challenged. And again, Billie Sol ended the challenge: "He's with me." After a short hop to another city, they met some of Billie Sol's business associates at the best restaurant in town. As they entered, Floyd was told, "Boy, go around to the back where you belong." Predictably by then, Billie Sol said, "No, he's with me." Over and over, in fancy restaurants and white-only hotels, Floyd heard those familiar words, "He's with me."

In a long telephone conversation with my friend and brother Floyd, he told me he had related some of these stories at Billie Sol's funeral, and summarized by saying, "Some glad morning when this life is over and I stand just outside the pearly gates and somebody says, 'Floyd doesn't deserve to come in here. Floyd isn't good enough. Floyd doesn't know enough. Floyd hasn't done enough,' I dream of hearing Jesus call from the other side, 'Open the gate; he is with me!'"

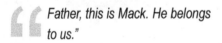
Father, this is Mack. He belongs to us."

When my brother-in-law, Dr. Mack Wayne Craig was near death, his daughter and her two brothers and I reflected on his life as we planned his funeral. They remembered their daddy saying many times, "My fondest ambition is to get to heaven, have Jesus take me by the arm, lead me to the throne, and say, 'Father, this is Mack. He belongs to us.'"

He's with me! He belongs to us! Encouraging Words!

" He provided redemption for his people; he ordained his covenant forever – holy and awesome is his name" (Psalm 111:9, NIV).

CHAPTER TWENTY-TWO

The Water Is Your Friend!

> " The best swimming teacher in the world lives just a couple of blocks from you!"

Miami, Florida is a city laced with canals, rivers, lakes, at least 70 public swimming pools, and more private pools than anyone can count, not to mention Biscayne Bay and the Atlantic Ocean. Mary Margaret and I knew it was no place for four young children who had not yet learned to swim. As we began asking about swimming instructors, one friend said, "Why, the best swimming teacher in the world lives just a couple of blocks from you!" How could we not consider the best?

> " George Le Duc took on the daunting task of teaching a champion swimmer how to swim better."

George Le Duc had gained fame during World War II teaching paraplegics to swim as part of their recovery. But George had known fame of a different sort years before the war. In 1932, Hollywood executives decided the Edgar Rice Burroughs stories about Tarzan had great movie potential. Johnny Weissmuller, who had won three gold medals for swimming in the 1924 Olympics and two more in the 1928 games, and was the holder of 67 world records, was their choice to be Tarzan.

Unfortunately, Weissmuller couldn't swim the way they wanted. He was a speed swimmer, but they needed a form swimmer, someone who could swim up to the shore with his broad chest halfway out of the water. George Le Duc took on the daunting task of teaching a champion swimmer how to swim better. Now, thirty years later, he was going to teach our kids!

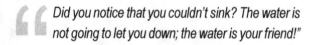

Did you notice that you couldn't sink? The water is not going to let you down; the water is your friend!"

George was a wizened old man, skin tanned like leather by long exposure to the Florida sun, and a cigarette always dangling from his lips. It was a race between lung cancer and skin cancer to see what would get him first, or if emphysema would beat them both.

George started by putting kids at ease when they came for their first swimming lesson. Standing in water that came up to eight-year-old Richard's chest, George fished in the pocket of his swim trunks and pulled out a shiny penny. "Oops, I dropped it and it went to the bottom. Richard, can you pick that up for me?" Richard bent over as he would on dry land, and was immediately horizontal on top of the water, unable to reach the penny, and unable to do anything but flounder. George gently set Richard back on his feet and said, "Did you notice that you couldn't sink? The water is not going to let you down; the water is your friend!"

Our children all became confident and accomplished

swimmers, thanks to the guy who taught Tarzan, and who taught our kids that "the water is your friend!"

> *She wanted so much to obey God, but it was with fear and trembling that she made her unsteady way down the steps and stood, shaking like a leaf."*

For about 50 years I didn't give those words any significance beyond the obvious. Then, a friend called one day to ask if I could help him baptize a man he had been teaching. When I got to the church building, I found a small crowd had gathered – friends, relatives, co-workers – and Kelly's mother, a woman about my age. As we went through the handshaking and getting acquainted time, I learned that the mother had tried for years to be baptized but was deathly afraid of water. As she told me of a childhood experience that had caused her unreasonable fear, her eyes filled with tears as she said, "I just wish I could be as brave as Kelly and be baptized today."

> *… we raised her from that watery grave and a radiant smile burst over, not just her face, but her whole being."*

Several times she affirmed her desire, and I assured her that if she really wanted to be baptized, we would help her. As I talked with her quietly and tried to assuage her fear, suddenly I remembered words from the past and said, "The water is your friend." Then I outlined a plan: "I'm going to baptize Kelly, and then he is going to stay in the water with me. He's going to get on one side, and I'll be on the other, and we'll baptize you if that's what you really want." "Oh yes," she said, "that's what I've wanted as long as I can remember!"

We helped her into the baptistery, I massaged her back and

shoulders to help her relax, and her son and I baptized her. When Sue died I was not able to travel for her funeral, but I wrote these lines: "She wanted so much to obey God, but it was with fear and trembling that she made her unsteady way down the steps and stood, shaking like a leaf. Until, that is, we raised her from that watery grave and a radiant smile burst over, not just her face, but her whole being." On that happy day, all her fears were laid to rest, and the water she had feared all her life had become her friend.

CHAPTER TWENTY-THREE

Daughter of the World

> Single-name identities are usually reserved for people in the sports or entertainment worlds, and they are awarded to those who have achieved stardom. An impressive teenage girl has changed those rules."

No basketball fan would ever ask, "Kareem who?" The same for Shaq, or LeBron, or Yogi (oops, he's baseball). How many Bono fans know or care that his birth name is Paul David Hewson? They should all be glad that he chose Bono (from bonavox, Latin for good voice) rather than sticking with his original one-word stage name: Steinhegvanhuysenolegbangbangbang! And who knows that Madonna was born Madonna Louise Ciccone?

> The extremists are afraid of books and pens. The power of education frightens them. They are afraid of women. The power of the voice of women frightens them."

Single-name identities are usually reserved for people in the sports or entertainment worlds, and they are awarded to those who have achieved stardom. An impressive teenage girl has changed those rules. At age 11 she was writing a blog for the BBC describing what life was like under the rule of the Taliban. The following year the New York Times produced a documentary about her efforts. On October 9, 2012, a Talib fighter jumped on a school bus in Mingora, Pakistan and shot his quarry in the head after she identified herself to spare her classmates. In a matter of hours, the whole world knew Malala.

Malala Yousafzai, born July 12, 1997, almost lost her life at the age of 15. But, after a series of surgeries and intense rehabilitation at Queen Elizabeth Hospital in Birmingham, England, she made a remarkable recovery. Her sixteenth birthday was celebrated at the United Nations in New York City. Former British Prime Minister Gordon Brown introduced Malala to an audience of more than 500 young people from 85 countries "with words the Taliban never wanted you to hear: Happy Sixteenth Birthday, Malala!"

As the U. N. Special Envoy for Global Education, Brown encouraged the creation of a special fund and a special goal to have all school-age children in school by the end of 2015. Malala, resplendent in a pink shawl once worn by former Pakistani President Benazir Bhutto, assassinated by Islamic extremists in 2007, was an eloquent spokesperson for the global cause. "The extremists are afraid of books and pens. The power of education frightens them. They are afraid of women. The power of the voice of women frightens them."

> *The places most desperately in need of education are the very places not getting it."*

UNESCO and Save the Children report that 28.5 million children in the world are not getting any primary school education. Ninety-five percent of these children live in low and lower-middle income countries, forty-four percent in sub-Sahara

Africa, nineteen percent in southwest Asia, and fourteen percent in Arab states. The places most desperately in need of education are the very places not getting it. In Malala's words, "One child, one teacher, one pen and one book can change the world. Education is the only solution. Education first."

Malala obviously speaks her native Pashto and is remarkably fluent in barely accented English. Her passion for education is understandable, given her background as the daughter of an educator who owns a chain of schools. Malala's father has described his daughter, born into a Sunni Muslim family, as "the daughter of the world." At times in her young life dreaming of being a doctor, a pilot, an educator, or a politician, Malala stands a good chance of being any or all the above. Yet she has reached this point despite unbelievable difficulties.

The Taliban have blown up more than a hundred girls' schools in Pakistan. They have so discouraged education for girls that only 70 of 700 girls enrolled were able to attend in Mingora. Conditions in Syria are even worse, with 3,900 schools destroyed in two years.

> *Weakness, fear, and hopelessness died. Strength, power, and courage were born."*

Bishop Desmond Tutu has honored Malala by nominating her for the International Children's Peace Prize. She was also nominated for and was awarded the Nobel Peace Prize, the youngest nominee and winner in the 119-year history of the award. At the end of 2012, Time magazine named her one of the 100 most influential people in the world, and she was one of four runners up for Time's Person of the Year award.

Neither her near-death experience nor the accolades of an adoring world appear to have lessened her determination. When asked to reflect on the assassination attempt, Malala said, "Nothing changed in my life except this: weakness, fear, and hopelessness died. Strength, power, and courage were born."

For some people, a single-name identity is enough.

Happy Birthday, Malala, daughter of the world!

CHAPTER TWENTY-FOUR

Shame in Black and White

The guest preacher had just been introduced and was beginning his sermon when the black man came into the all-white church service. When he started toward an empty seat, an usher stepped up, whispered in the African American man's ear, produced a folding chair, and seated him all alone in the lobby.

The visiting minister was confused by what he saw, puzzled as to why the black worshipper would abide such treatment, and upset with himself for not speaking out against what appeared to be blatant segregation. But he rationalized that maybe he had misinterpreted what he saw; the visitor may have had good reasons of his own to stay and, besides, a guest speaker should not be rude to his hosts.

How do I know all this? I was that guest preacher, and I have lived for many years with the shame and conviction that I should not have let the incident pass unchallenged, or at least unquestioned.

America remains two societies – one black and one white – and that is nowhere more evident than in our churches. Much has changed since Gunnar Myrdal's monumental study of racism in America, but too little has been corrected. In most communities, we have achieved too little integration in our churches, and we will make little progress in the future if we just let our sinful nature run its course.

Most church folks wouldn't know Richard Price or his novel *Clockers,* the story of black teen cocaine dealers and the white police who do battle with them. A former cocaine addict himself, Price spent many months with drug dealers and cops alike. His 1992 book and the 1995 movie directed by Spike Lee caused *Time* magazine to conclude: "Price took the trouble to find out and returned from his voyage of discovery with an overpowering portrait of a grim and neglected world."

Racism is not our only social injustice, but it may be the longest lingering and the most visible. The time for us to take our own voyage of discovery and commit ourselves to change is long overdue.

The small town where I grew up in Tennessee was built on the banks of the Cumberland River. On Riverside Drive were large houses where the plant manager and other executives lived. As one moved farther away from the river, the houses became smaller and were occupied by workers rather than executives. Eventually one came to the spur railroad track and, literally, on the other side of the track was a small group of houses we called "colored town" when we wanted to be polite. Born in the white part of town, I lived there until I graduated from college and moved away. In all those years, I never once set foot in the black part of town. I never knew a person who lived there, never went to church with anybody who lived there, never went to school, never had any interaction at all.

We felt magnanimous because they had their own church and their own school. Why, we even gave them our worn-out hymnals and Sunday School chairs! Is it any wonder that a generation arose that said, "Enough?" The wonder is that it took so long for people to rebel, and that many of us were so tone deaf when they did. One might argue that the end of lynching and Jim Crow laws represented progress, but dehumanizing people of color has not disappeared.

More than a century ago, David Lipscomb wrote in the February 1878 *Gospel Advocate:* "We believe it is sinful to have two congregations in the same community for persons of separate and distinct races. That race prejudice would cause trouble in the churches we know. It did this in apostolic days. Not once did the apostles suggest that they should form separate congregations for the different races. But they always admonished them to unity, forbearance, love, and brotherhood in Jesus Christ."

We haven't changed all that much in the 142 years since Lipscomb wrote those words. Neither the inactivity of neglect nor the hyperactivity of ambitious social engineering is working well. Maybe we don't know how to change the world – or even the church – but we can change ourselves. We can learn to see all people as brothers and sisters made in the image of God. If we will sow that seed of good will, He will provide the harvest.

> *Let the redeemed of the Lord tell their story – those he redeemed from the hand of the foe"* (Psalm 107:2, NIV).

CHAPTER TWENTY-FIVE

Mine's Got a Popsicle in It!

> *Both Yanks and Rebs had camped in that building, carving their initials in the homemade poplar benches that passed for pews."*

The country congregation would have been larger if people could have found the church building. Even that unflappable woman in my GPS who calmly tells me she's "Recalculating, Recalculating" would have lost her cool trying to find that place.

> *Mary Margaret and I, already planning to be married after we graduated the following year, decided that little church needed a Vacation Bible School."*

The paved road gave way to gravel that gave way to dirt that ended at a creek you dared not try to ford after a hard rain. But if you finally overcame those hurdles, and there was nowhere else to go, there it was – a once-white clapboard structure built before the Civil War.

Both "Yanks" and "Rebs" had camped in that building, carving their initials in the homemade poplar benches that passed for pews. There was no plumbing, and of course no air-conditioning. Open windows without screens were an invitation to flies, mosquitoes, even birds that were not reluctant to express their opinion of the preaching.

I had started preaching as a high school boy, "circuit-riding" to a different place each Sunday of the month so I didn't have to prepare new sermons every week. Now, in my junior year of college, I had graduated to preaching every Sunday at the same place.

> *When I popped the top and handed a drink to a little girl, she turned it up and screamed, 'Mine's got a popsicle in it!'"*

In the summer following our junior year, Mary Margaret and I, already planning to be married after we graduated the following year, decided that little church needed a Vacation Bible School. Many of the people had no transportation, and it would be hard to divide into classes in that one-room building, but that did not dampen our enthusiasm at all.

Providing refreshments was a different story. An old farmer had the solution if we could only implement it.

He said:

> *You get you a number two warshtub, a big block of ice (no cubes in neat plastic bags back then), some ice cream salt, and some Nehis (Nehi was the local brand of the "big orange drank" that Andy Griffith had described in his early comedy routines). You chip up the ice, put down a layer, then a layer of salt, then the Nehis, and keep doing that 'til the tub is full."*

He cautioned that the timing had to be just right or the drinks would freeze and pop off the bottle caps or, worse, cause the bottles to break.

We gave it a try. When I popped the top and handed a drink to a little girl, she turned it up and screamed, "Mine's got a popsicle in it!" I'll never forget how her eyes sparkled and her face filled with delight at the unexpected pleasure.

> *The woman asked, 'Would you mind telling me where that popsicle incident occurred?' When I told her, she smiled and said, 'I thought so; I'm that little girl...'"*

Years later, I was preaching somewhere and told that story to illustrate the joy of unexpected blessings or serendipities. Afterwards, a woman stood off to the side, and when the crowd thinned, she came to me and asked, "Would you mind telling me where that popsicle incident occurred?" When I told her, she smiled and said, "I thought so; I'm that little girl, and I'd like you to meet my husband and children." I smiled and thought, "Better than a popsicle!"

During that VBS week, I stopped at a farm home to see if two little girls could come for classes the next day. The mom came to the door and unleashed a tirade that left me speechless. No, her girls wouldn't be going to VBS, and they were planning to change churches because of this man, that woman, this policy, that procedure, etc. When I got back to my car, already discouraged, I found that a tire had gone flat. There I was, on a hot summer day, in front of a house where not even the dog liked me. I wasn't a member of AAA, but they couldn't have found me anyway. That day there was nothing to do but roll up my sleeves and change the tire.

After a few minutes, the mom brought me a glass of cold lemonade. I don't know if it was a peace offering or an apology, but it certainly was a refreshing serendipity. I do know that the girls went to Vacation Bible School and Sunday School, and that I later had the honor of baptizing the husband and father and forming a lasting friendship.

I hope this is a good day for you. But if the problems overwhelm you, the hurt won't go away, the sickness is not responding to treatment, the conflict just won't be resolved, just keep on lickin' because there's a popsicle in your day somewhere!

CHAPTER TWENTY-SIX

It's an Absolute Joy!

> *Our marriage was a partnership, my brawn and her brains."*

As we neared our 58th wedding anniversary, Mary Margaret and I shared our concerns that we couldn't do all the things we used to do. We talked about how our marriage was a partnership, my brawn and her brains, and if her brain was as weak as my brawn we were in big trouble!

She was particularly upset that I had to do some of the things she had always done. "Whoa!" I said. "Stop right there. What if our situations were reversed and I could no longer drive the car, or take out the trash, or shop for groceries…?" She smiled – barely – and said, "Well, I guess I would do the best I can, but it wouldn't be much fun!" I agreed. "No, it isn't always fun, but it's an absolute joy every day!"

> *It may not be a formula for fun, but it's a sure-fire way to guarantee joy."*

Fun is centered on self. Joy is centered on others.

Someone said to me, "I've been taking care of other people for a long time; from now on I'm going to take care of me!" I opined that every person must make his or her own choice about that, but my greatest happiness has come when I focused on others rather than myself. Years ago, I saw an acronym that I've always liked:

J – Jesus first
O – Others second
Y – Yourself last

It may not be a formula for fun, but it's a sure-fire way to guarantee joy.

Fun was not the focus of Jesus' life, but joy was, all the way to the end. Speaking of the race we are running as we live out our time on earth, a preacher of long ago encouraged,

> Let us fix our eyes on Jesus... the author and perfecter of our faith, who for the joy set before him endured the cross, scorning its shame, ...and sat down at the right hand of the throne of God" (Hebrews 12:2, BSB).

That was no amusement park atop Mt. Calvary; it was not a fun place to be. But Jesus found joy there as he fulfilled his mission for others – for me!

For a long time, I didn't want to hear these words from Jesus:

> Whoever wants to be great must become a servant... Whoever wants to be first among you must be your slave. That is what the Son of Man has done: He came to serve, not to be served – ...and then to give away his life in exchange for many who are held hostage" (Mark 10:45, MSG).

So that's why my friend had business cards identifying him as "Servant of Christ – How may I serve you?" He came to serve, not to be served.

The year was 1985, and my Sunday School class had assembled as usual, visiting, laughing, drinking coffee. But one man was somber and a bit angry. "What's with you people?" he demanded. "Don't you know that a major earthquake devastated Mexico City last night, killing at least 10,000 and maybe as many as 40,000 people? Shouldn't we at least be praying about that, and maybe taking up a contribution to help?"

> *This morning I gave it all, and I have never felt so good about myself!"*

Considerably subdued, we paused for prayer, then passed around the top of a donut box into which people put more than $2,000 for Mexico City relief efforts. After class, a lady came to me with her wallet in her hand and tears in her eyes. Opening an empty compartment, she said, "This is where I keep my mad money – money I may need for emergencies or special wants. This morning I gave it all, and I have never felt so good about myself!"

People looking only for fun can find it, but they stop occasionally to wonder, "Is this all there is?" People looking for joy can also find it, but not in the mirror, not in self, but in service to God and others. Is there something in your life that is an absolute joy every day?

> *I have swept away your offenses like a cloud, your sins like the morning mist. Return to me, for I have redeemed you"* (Isaiah 44:22, NIV).

CHAPTER TWENTY-SEVEN

By the Grace of God

> *His voice was so deep it rumbled like a semi using a jake brake on a downgrade."*

The guy was BIG. I mean pro football, defensive tackle big… and he was black… and he was a preacher… and he was my partner as we worked on a Habitat for Humanity house that hot Saturday in August. I don't know why we were paired together – perhaps because nobody else wanted to work with a preacher – or maybe because I had worked on Habitat houses before. We were about as different as two men could be. If we had been singing, I would have been the high tenor while he sang bass an octave low. His voice was so deep it rumbled like a semi using a jake brake on a downgrade.

> *Well, if that's your story, you better stick to it, but I thought I heard something."*

We worked well together, getting a lot done that morning. We were tentative with one another, feeling each other out, searching for a comfort level. All that changed when we took our lunch break. After going through the line and filling our plates with barbeque and beans, we made ourselves as comfortable as we could while sitting on piles of building materials.

Just when I got my mouth full of barbeque, my new friend suddenly grew talkative. Putting on his best imitation cotton-field voice, he rumbled, "Has you ever noticed how white folks and black folks smell pretty much the same once we gits all hot and stinky?" I finally managed to quit coughing and sputtering, and got my food going the right direction when he hit me again.

> *If you are ready to be baptized, you need to find somebody else to help you, because right now, I'd hold you under so long the only music you'd hear would be harps and trumpets!"*

"And has you noticed," he said, "that Methodist preachers and Church of Christ preachers say pretty much the same thing when we hit our thumbs with a hammer?" Not quite so unprepared this time, I said, "I didn't really say a bad word, did I?" His deep belly laugh made my teeth vibrate, and he said, "Well, if that's your story, you better stick to it, but I thought I heard something."

He had one more zinger for me: "I bet it would really make your day if you could get this old boy straightened out on baptism and music." "Listen," I said, trying to get back in the game, "if you are ready to be baptized, you need to find somebody else to help you, because right now, I'd hold you under so long the only music you'd hear would be harps and trumpets!" The ground shook again as he laughed like Fat Albert and said, "You know somethin'? You all right… unless you hits your thumb again!"

> *Church may be where the gospel is preached, but the world is where the gospel is lived."*

Right after lunch my new friend disappeared. I found him on his hands and knees, writing scripture verses and short prayers with a magic marker. I had told him church volunteers often wrote like that on parts of the house that would be covered with finish materials. He had selected the sub-floor as his place to write. At first, I thought he was so big he was having trouble getting up. Then I realized he was not only writing the prayers; he was praying the prayers. I introduced him to the woman whose family would live in that home. She was fulfilling the "sweat equity" required of all Habitat homeowners, who continue to do volunteer work after their own home is completed. When she asked why we were volunteering on such a hot day, we just said, "Because Jesus would."

At the end of the long, hot day, when my ten-pound tool belt felt like fifty, I trudged almost half a mile to where my truck was parked. Easing my aching muscles into the driver's seat, I realized I had seen and lived the gospel that day, and I hadn't even been to church. Church may be where the gospel is preached, but the world is where the gospel is lived.

Church has been my life, but I'm not sure Jesus likes that. He didn't spend much time in the pulpit, but he did his preaching from a boat, on a mountain side, in a living room in Bethany, by a well in Samaria. If he were alive today, is it possible he would choose an unfinished Habitat house for his pulpit?

My new friend suddenly had a soft voice that didn't rumble. "You're all right," he said. As I began to protest, he added, "by the grace of God, you're all right." I could accept that, gratefully realizing that no other power in the world could make me all right. By the grace of God!

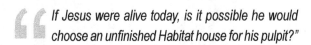
If Jesus were alive today, is it possible he would choose an unfinished Habitat house for his pulpit?"

> *Jesus Christ is both the only price and sacrifice by which eternal redemption is obtained for believers"* (Jonathan Edwards).

CHAPTER TWENTY-EIGHT

My Certainty for Your Uncertainty?

> " *No one has done enough; no one is good enough to go to Heaven. We don't get to Heaven because we have performed a long list of good works; we get to Heaven by the grace of God."*

As my mother neared the end of her life, her comments sometimes bordered on the comical, but most of the time they were painfully serious. I had to smile a bit when she said, "I'm not afraid to die, but I don't really know what it's like because I've never been dead!"

> " *I finally left with the painful feeling that I had raised her anxiety rather than her confidence."*

But I wasn't smiling on another day when my sadness was more like grief. I visited Mother to give comfort and assurance, but on this day, I unintentionally added to her anxiety.

"Do you think," she asked, "that I have really done enough, that I have been good enough, to go to Heaven?" Completely misreading the situation, I thought she had given me an opening to preach a sermonette about grace. "No, Mother," I said, "No one has done enough; no one is good enough to go to Heaven. We don't get to Heaven because we have performed a long list of good works; we get to Heaven by the grace of God."

A few more sentences and I suddenly realized from my mother's expression that she wasn't hearing a word I said. She had heard only the first sentence of my answer: "No, Mother. No one has done enough; no one is good enough to go to Heaven." Of course, I tried to explain, to be sure she understood, to build her trust. But I finally left with the painful feeling that I had raised her anxiety rather than her confidence.

> *It isn't arrogance at all; it's assurance – blessed assurance!"*

A veteran preacher was teaching a class on Christian confidence and assurance. A class member became increasingly uncomfortable with what he thought was spiritual arrogance. He asked, "Are you saying that you know that if you die right now, you'll go to Heaven? Isn't that terribly arrogant?" With a confident twinkle in his eye, the old preacher said, "Of course that's what I'm saying. And it isn't arrogance at all; it's assurance – blessed assurance!"

My friend Ray Hawk knew a man who had a donut shop where he displayed some pamphlets Ray had written. One day a woman picked up a paper, read it hurriedly, and asked the proprietor, "Do you really believe what's in here?" When he assured her that he did believe, she said, "I have just one question. If you die right now, will you go to Heaven?" When he began to equivocate and mumble an "I hope so" answer, she smiled and said, "I don't think I want to swap my certainty for your uncertainty!"

> We neither make nor save ourselves. God does both the making and the saving."

I knew another preacher who would say to his audience, "I want you to have a faith so strong that you know that you know that you know you are saved!"

If Robert Fulghum really learned everything he needed to know in kindergarten, why did he pursue higher education at Baylor University? Human knowledge is constantly being revised as new information becomes known. Faith in God is constantly growing as our relationship with him grows.

I had my epiphany as a young preacher when I delivered a sermon chastising people for not doing more and working harder to assure their salvation. In what I am convinced was a providential choice, the song following my sermon said, "Jesus paid it all, all to him I owe…." Because I owe that debt, I live a life of faith, expressing my gratitude every day for the price of my redemption he paid at Calvary.

We are uncertain when we trust in ourselves and worry about our performance. When we trust in Him, we gratefully accept the fullness of redemption. Eugene Peterson has captured the essence of the Apostle Paul's message to Christians in Ephesus:

> Saving is all his idea, and all his work… All we do is trust him enough to let him do it. It's God's gift from start to finish! We don't play the major role. If we did, we'd probably go around bragging that we'd done the whole thing! No, we neither make nor save ourselves. God

> does both the making and the saving. He creates each of us by Christ Jesus to join him in the work he does, the good work he has gotten ready for us to do, ...work we had better be doing" (Ephesians 2:8,9, MSG).

His certainty or your uncertainty. The gift is His; the choice is yours.

CHAPTER TWENTY-NINE

Beauty Is not Always Pretty

> " Some wear rough, crude emblems of His suffering while others wear precious-metal, jewel-encrusted symbols of His sacrifice."

Is the cross of Jesus Christ the ugliest, or the most beautiful object in all history? The answer depends on one's perspective. Rough, nail-scarred, blood-stained wood, symbolizing every wrong, every injustice, every indignity one could imagine… how could it be described as anything but ugly? But, on the other hand, because it symbolizes God's love for his people and represents the ultimate sacrifice freely given… how could it be described as anything but beautiful?

> " I realized how truly alone my friend was, and how completely surrounded by friends and family I was. Life is beautiful."

People who wear crucifixes don't seem able to resolve this question. Some wear rough, crude emblems of His suffering while others wear precious-metal, jewel-encrusted symbols of His sacrifice. Whether it's made of rough wood or precious metal, I'll argue for the beauty of the cross.

On the Sunday after my father had died on a Saturday, I was both grieving for my loss and rejoicing in his victory. When I spoke to a man at church who had left the best of his body and mind on a battlefield in Korea, he told me how sad he was because his dog had died the day before. My first reaction was resentment. My dad and your dog? Come on! Then I realized how truly alone my friend was, and how completely surrounded by friends and family I was. Life is beautiful.

Mat Dawson could have retired to a comfortable pension years earlier. But at age seventy-eight, he was still driving his 1985 Ford Escort, living in a one-bedroom apartment, and still driving a forklift at Ford Motor Company where he had worked for fifty-nine years. He even worked overtime to boost his earnings. Why? So he could add to the more than a million dollars he had given to schools and charities since 1994. Not bad for a guy who dropped out of school in the seventh grade! Life is beautiful.

Sarah Andrews was just a teenager when she asked her family to support her missionary dreams rather than bankroll a wedding. She took the message of Jesus to Japan, and stayed there through the terrifying years of World War II.

> "She shared her daily bowl of rice with fellow-prisoners weaker and sicker than she. 'I've gone without food,' she said, 'but I've never been hungry.' Life is beautiful."

Imprisoned and tortured, she shared her daily bowl of rice with fellow-prisoners weaker and sicker than she. "I've gone without food," she said, "but I've never been hungry." Life is beautiful.

Corrie ten Boom and her sister Betsie fretted about the fleas that infested their German concentration camp barracks until they learned that the guards in other buildings were systematically raping and torturing the women, while sparing Corrie and Betsie because of the fleas. They thanked God for the fleas, his blessing of protection. Life is beautiful.

Abraham and Moses had passed retirement age (at least by twenty-first century American standards) when God called them to further service. Despite the hardships and disappointments they encountered, we remember them for their faithful partnership with God. Life is beautiful.

> When the blanket was pulled back, the baby's face was a picture of peace, contentment, security, and hope. Even in the midst of terror, life is beautiful."

Esther, having become queen of Persia, could have forgotten her oppressed Jewish people and lived a life of ease, but she had been elevated to a place of honor in the kingdom for a godly purpose, a purpose that she was determined to fulfill regardless of personal risk. She was beautiful and so was her life.

A national magazine cover pictured a refugee mother fleeing Kosovo, clutching her suckling baby to her breast. On the mother's face was written pain, anguish, even terror. But when the blanket was pulled back, the baby's face was a picture of peace, contentment, security, and hope. Even in the midst of terror, life is beautiful.

Have you suffered unbearable loss? Has life become so ugly you can hardly face it?

Your life may not always be pretty, but it can always be beautiful!

> *The cost of redemption cannot be overstated. The wonders of grace cannot be overemphasized. Christ took the hell he didn't deserve so we could have the heaven we don't deserve"* (Randy Alcorn).

CHAPTER THIRTY

When America Became a Church

> "We just have a report from our correspondent Dan Rather in Dallas, that he has confirmed President Kennedy is dead." — Walter Cronkite

I was in a barber shop at the corner of N. W. 27th Avenue and N. W. 7th Street in Miami, Florida. The Cuban refugee who cut my hair regularly would never give me any name but Joe, and there was no visible license to identify him otherwise. I insisted that he call me Phillip, but he insisted on calling me Father.

There was the usual barber shop banter – sports, politics – mostly gossip of the male variety. During lulls in the conversation, the black and white television would blare out a reminder of its presence. Everybody who walked by felt obligated to tweak the rabbit-ears antenna in the hope of getting more than a snowstorm. Every time a barber turned his clippers on or off, the TV picture would roll and break up into geometric patterns more interesting than the soap opera everybody ignored.

> "Although he was known as the most trusted man in America, Cronkite's news that day was unbelievable."

The afternoon routine was suddenly shattered by the announcement of a news bulletin and the familiar voice of Walter Cronkite. Although he was known as the most trusted man in America, Cronkite's news that day was unbelievable: "Three shots were fired at President Kennedy's motorcade in downtown Dallas. The first reports say that President Kennedy has been seriously wounded." The shop grew quiet, the conversation subdued, as if we knew the later news bulletins before we heard them: "We just have a report from our correspondent Dan Rather in Dallas, that he has confirmed President Kennedy is dead."

I paid Joe for my haircut and began to walk a couple of blocks to Kensington Park Elementary School where our oldest son had started first grade a few weeks earlier. We had walked with him the first few days, and then let him walk with friends or by himself. He felt really grown up when he pushed the button that turned the light red and stopped traffic so people could cross the busy street.

On this afternoon, I watched as he pushed the button and got halfway across the street before he looked up and saw me. Assuming I had come to walk him home, he began yelling, "What are you doing here? I'm a big boy! I can walk home by myself!" When I told him President Kennedy had been killed, he began asking the why question we still can't answer and the who question some people still think we can't answer.

Everyone old enough to remember the assassination of our 35th president has his or her own memory of that day fifty-seven years ago, November 22, 1963.

> *It was almost as if the whole people bowed their head and America, for a time, became a church."*

Time seemed to stand still that Friday afternoon. The Thanksgiving sermon I had prepared for the next Sunday no longer seemed appropriate. Many businesses closed. Even Jack Ruby, a man nobody knew on Friday, but everybody would know on Sunday, closed his Dallas nightclub. George Cornell, religion writer for the Associated Press, said "It was almost as if the whole people bowed their head and America, for a time, became a church." Other observers said that more Americans attended church that Sunday than on any other day in American history.

> *...evil deeds are often done in the name of righteousness."*

Jack Ruby took matters into his own hands that Sunday when he shot and killed Lee Harvey Oswald, the accused assassin. Other people expressed their outrage in less violent ways. When Dallas businessman and civic leader Stanley Marcus sought to calm his city, he received hundreds of protest letters, many of them containing no-longer-wanted Neiman Marcus credit cards.

I reminded my church audience that Sunday that tragedy is a great equalizer, and that evil deeds are often done in the name of righteousness. For the fourth time in our nation's history, all of us joined in mourning the death of a president. Abraham Lincoln was the first, killed by John Wilkes Booth in 1865. Just sixteen years later, in 1881, James A. Garfield was killed by Charles Jules Guiteau. Twenty years later, in 1901, it was William McKinley who was killed by Leon Czolgosz, and now, John Fitzgerald Kennedy. Booth claimed to be punishing a tyrant; Guiteau claimed to be acting "for the good of the country and at the command of God."

Please, God, bless America, guard us against such pseudo-patriots, and, without our having to experience such unspeakable tragedy, help America to become a church once again.

CHAPTER THIRTY-ONE

You've Got a Lifetime Guarantee!

> *Can you imagine how many times in more than 50 years of ministry I've heard the I-got-it-all speech?"*

My surgeon grew up in a small town in Tennessee but did his training at one of the most prestigious hospitals in New York City. He could be country boy in one instant and suave sophisticate in the next. When he came into the recovery room while I was still groggy from the anesthesia, he was pure country boy. "You got cancer," he boomed, making me wonder if he missed class the day they studied bedside manner. "But you're gonna be fine," he continued, "it was small and contained and I got it all." He looked startled when I began to laugh and asked, "Bernie, can you imagine how many times in more than 50 years of ministry I've heard the I-got-it-all speech?"

> *I feel so confident that I'm gonna give you a guarantee – a lifetime guarantee – You're gonna live 'til you die!"*

"Yeah," he said, "I see your point. But this time I really mean it. I took out a section of your colon just to be sure, and then I sewed you back together. I feel so confident that I'm gonna give you a guarantee – a lifetime guarantee – You're gonna live 'til you die!" Wow! I thought, there's a guarantee I can understand. No fine print, no caveats, no mystery. I'm going to live until I die. The operation and the conversation took place more than twenty years ago, and so far, the guarantee is holding!

Considering the number of people I have known who stopped living before they died, "Live 'til you die" strikes me as a good motto. Ariel Sharon, the former Prime Minister of Israel, suffered a massive stroke on January 4, 2006 and was in a coma for eight years before dying.

I don't have a right to question decisions made by Sharon's family and doctors, but I do have the right to say that I don't want to live like that. Mary Margaret and I have made living wills and signed medical directives that we hope will prevent such an occurrence. I tell doctors, "I am a reasonably active and alert 80-year-old man who has no intention of being a 90-year-old vegetable. You have no obligation to keep me alive forever; I've got that covered!"

Time magazine (January 20, 2014) had an article by Andy Crouch, executive editor of Christianity Today. Crouch pointed out that modern technology has given new meaning to the "valley of the shadow of death." It is often people of faith, believing in God's power to heal miraculously, who are the most reluctant to let their loved ones pass through the valley. It takes strong faith to believe in the power of prayer to heal the sick. It takes even stronger faith to believe that what awaits us at the other end of the valley is more wonderful than anything we have known in this life.

Of course, there's nothing novel about the promise and nothing unique about my guarantee. We like to pretend that somehow we're going to beat the odds and prove the insurance actuaries wrong. But we can't escape what someone has called the ultimate statistic: one out of one dies. Even Jesus – all human, all divine, and all powerful – could not escape the appointment all must keep. He overcame death in his resurrection, but not until he had felt its sting in the most cruel and painful death imaginable.

> *Jesus had the ultimate defense that prevailed against the ultimate weapon."*

Satan tempted Jesus in the wilderness, but our Lord resisted hunger, power, honor, and every other temptation the devil could concoct. Matthew simply says,

> *...the devil left him, and angels came and attended him" (Matthew 4:11, NIV).*

But Satan did not know he was defeated. He still had in his arsenal the ultimate weapon of death, the great equalizer that stops all human activity. Jesus had the ultimate defense that prevailed against the ultimate weapon. His resurrection power is not his alone, but also our victory that overcomes even death. For us as well as Jesus,

> *The last enemy that shall be destroyed is death" (1 Corinthians 15:26, KJV).*

At hospital and hospice bedsides I am often asked to recite the twenty-third Psalm. On every such occasion I remember an old story about a social gathering attended by both a famous actor and an old preacher. After the actor had regaled the audience with recitations of several famous works, the old preacher asked him to recite the twenty-third Psalm.

The actor agreed if the preacher would also recite the Psalm. The actor's rendition was flawless, and the audience applauded politely. The old preacher's voice cracked, and his recitation was far from perfect, but the audience applauded wildly, and everyone had tears in their eyes.

Asked to explain the difference in reaction, the actor said simply, "I know the Psalm, but my friend knows the Shepherd."

CHAPTER THIRTY-TWO

Are You Ready for Some Football?

> *As a fan, I have become an enabler for what is a national obsession if not a national obscenity."*

I never earned a football letter or team jacket, but I did get a splinter from the far end of my high school junior varsity bench. That's why my picture in the yearbook is with the band rather than the football team.

Despite my inauspicious beginning, I became a fan wherever I was. In Detroit it was sitting in old Briggs Stadium watching the Detroit Lions play on the field they shared with the baseball Tigers. In Miami it was season tickets for Miami Hurricanes games in the old Orange Bowl with about thirty other young rowdies from our church, and, in that same stadium, watching the first game ever for the Miami Dolphins when hometown boy Joe Auer ran the opening kickoff back 95 yards for a touchdown.

> *It was heady stuff to have only a plate glass window between me and the owner's suite and celebrity guests like Ted Kennedy and Henry Kissinger."*

In Washington I had a friend who was a friend of Redskins Coach George Allen's wife. When her suite was not full, I would sometimes get to take the extra seat. It was heady stuff to have only a plate glass window between me and the owner's suite and celebrity guests like Ted Kennedy and Henry Kissinger. In Nashville I was an eyewitness to history when Bud Adams moved the Houston Oilers to town, and they became the Tennessee Titans.

I was in Neyland Stadium with a hundred thousand of my closest friends that glorious, cold, rainy Saturday afternoon in 1998 when the Arkansas quarterback fumbled, and the Tennessee Vols recovered to win the game, preserve their undefeated season, and eventually win the national championship.

As a fan, I have become an enabler for what is a national obsession if not a national obscenity. The word obscene occurred to me back around Super Bowl Thirty (Super Bowl XXX in NFLese) when all those Xs looked like something not usually associated with football. For one thing, the ticket prices are obscene. One reseller had 3,837 tickets available for Super Bowl XLVIII, ranging from $1,468 in the nosebleed section to $640,178 (I kid you not; look it up) for a suite somebody's not using. Something is really out of kilter when the head football coach at your state university is paid ten times more than the university president and substantially more than the governor.

The 58 Super Bowl TV ads sell for an average of $4 million per 30-second spot. City water departments have learned that water usage peaks during the ads, apparently because everybody is flushing at the same time.

> *After the most incredible game in school history, the Olivet players revealed they had planned and practiced a play designed not to score."*

Now that I've established my credentials as a fanatic, I want to join those who pick the most valuable this and the number one that for a recent season. My choice for the Team of the Year? Olivet Middle School in Olivet, Michigan. My choice for Play of the Year? The unlikely touchdown scored by the Olivet team. My choice for Player of the Year? Keith Orr of the Olivet team. My choice for Sportsmen of the Year? The entire Olivet team.

After the most incredible game in school history, the Olivet players revealed they had planned and practiced a play designed not to score. As they neared the goal line, the ball was pitched out to a running back whose blockers sealed off the defense and left a clear path to a touchdown. With no defensive player within ten yards, the running back stopped at the one-yard line, put the ball on the ground, and held it there until the whistle signaled that the play was over. Fans and coaches alike were baffled, but the Olivet team huddled near the ball, snapped it again, and moved, still in a huddle, across the goal line. The referee signaled a touchdown and the players ran to the sideline. Only then did the crowd and the coaches know that Keith Orr had been in the middle of the pack and had scored the only touchdown of his career.

> I kind of went from being somebody who mostly cared about me and my friends to caring about everyone and trying to make everyone's day and everyone's life."

Keith Orr was the smallest person on the team. He had significant learning disabilities and physical challenges that kept him from ever being a skilled athlete. But he also had a team of middle school buddies who wanted him to succeed. Without telling the coaches or asking permission, the team cooked up that special play for Keith.

Words can't really tell the story. To get the full impact, go to YouTube and watch the CBS News video. Watch all three minutes and forty-one seconds, because you don't want to miss teammate Justice Miller explain, as tears trickle down his cheeks, "I kind of went from being somebody who mostly cared about myself and my friends to caring about everyone and trying to make everyone's day and everyone's life."

CHAPTER THIRTY-THREE

My Life My Argument

> *We dreamed that our debate experience would equip us for ministry, for, after all, had not God's prophet said, 'Come now, and let us reason together...'" (Isaiah 1:18)?*

He was a fresh-out-of-college, first-year teacher at our small high school. Hired to teach English, he was also determined to build a debate team to compete with other schools. He picked class salutatorian Joel Lee to supply the brains and me, I suppose, to supply the mouth. To our surprise, we enjoyed a bit of success because Barney Crockerall was a great teacher. I give him all the credit for bringing focus to my argumentative nature.

> *Your argument that trumps my argument is still an argument, and I wanted ministry to be more than that."*

After that one senior year, Joel went on to a career in medicine and I in ministry. My college debate colleague was Robert McGowan who left after our freshman year to pursue a career in law. For the last three years my partner was fellow ministerial student Don McWhorter. We dreamed that our debate experience would equip us for ministry, for, after all, had not God's prophet said, "Come now, and let us reason together..." (Isaiah 1:18, KJV)? Interscholastic debate is about assembling arguments in favor of a proposition, then developing arguments to deny the same proposition. But it is not a search for truth. Your argument that trumps my argument is still an argument, and I wanted ministry to be more than that.

> *I have discovered that people don't care how much I know until they know how much I care."*

I was drinking coffee in Detroit one day with my closest preacher friend at the time and expressing my frustration. Ernie Stewart, in his calm yet direct way said, "Phil, I have discovered that people don't care how much I know until they know how much I care." I'd heard that statement before, and I've heard it many times since, but it has never impacted me as much as it did that day, probably because that was also the day Ernie told me he was leaving his ministry in Dearborn and he and Mary Frances were uprooting their family to move to Jerusalem to preach the message Jesus had preached there twenty centuries before. Ernie went with a head full of arguments but a heart full of caring.

> *Instead of trying to get acceptance of my ideas, I decided I would try to make my life my argument...."*

About that same time, I became interested in the life and work of a man who was born 145 years ago and died 55 years ago. Albert Schweitzer was born in Germany, the son of a Lutheran pastor. Schweitzer gained fame as a theologian, an organist, a philosopher, a physician, and a medical missionary. As a student of religion, he earned the Ph. D. degree at the University of Tubingen in 1899 when he was only 24.

At the age of 30, he was denied a place on a medical mission team because he lacked qualifications. So, he entered medical school and spent eight years pursuing his degree and practical training. His medical education was financed largely by income from his organ recitals featuring the works of Johann Sebastian Bach. In 1912, he and his wife Helene moved to Lambarene in what is now Gabon, (then a French colony in West Africa) and began their hospital in a converted chicken coop.

The world took notice of his work when he was awarded the Nobel Peace Prize in 1952. In 1957 a professor in France challenged his students to "define the last hope for the culture of Western Europe." A nineteen-year-old student said, "It is not in any part of Europe. It is in a small African village and it can be identified with an eighty-two-year-old man."

When American journalist Norman Cousins visited Lambarene and told Schweitzer that story, the old doctor was silent for long moments while he reflected on his life and then said, "In the morning when the sun is up and I hear the cries of the hospital, I do not think of these lofty ideals, but when the hospital is asleep, it means much to me that the students should believe these things. Instead of trying to get acceptance of my ideas, I decided I would try to make my life my argument…." My life my argument! What a novel idea! Or is it?

What can I learn from a German Lutheran who denied the existence of the historical Jesus I worship and adore? I learn from Schweitzer what I learn from Jesus: "The Son of Man did not come to be served, but to serve…" (Matthew 20:28, NIV). "Oh, to be like Thee! blessed Redeemer: This is my constant longing and prayer; Gladly I'll forfeit all of earth's treasures, Jesus, Thy perfect likeness to wear."

No doubt about it – he'll redeem Israel, buy back Israel from captivity to sin" (Psalm 130:8, MSG).

CHAPTER THIRTY-FOUR

If Necessary, Use Words

> My vision of long-haired hippies singing radical music faded as I listened, and I sheepishly said to Richard, 'Let's leave it on your station a little bit longer.'"

The death six years ago of 94-year-old folk singer Pete Seeger reminded me of one of my most embarrassing moments as a father. Late in the 1960s, or maybe in the early '70s, our oldest son got in the car with me and immediately changed the radio station from "my" music to "his" music.

I reacted as generations of parents have:

> Put that back on a good station; I can't stand that stuff." But Dad, just listen. "I don't want to listen to that garbage. I can't even understand what they are saying." Dad, just listen. "I told you I don't want to listen; change the station!" Dad, you don't have to like it, but I wish you would just listen."

After three or four exchanges, I decided to listen for a moment to satisfy my son. What I heard was the reason for my embarrassment.

To everything – Turn, Turn, Turn
There is a season – Turn, Turn, Turn
And a time for every purpose under heaven

A time to be born, a time to die
A time to plant, a time to reap
A time to kill, a time to heal
A time to laugh, a time to weep

Straight out of the Bible… the Old Testament book of Ecclesiastes… possibly written by the wise man Solomon, though scholars are not sure. My vision of long-haired hippies singing radical music faded as I listened, and I sheepishly said to Richard, "Let's leave it on your station a little bit longer."

A guy who is a child of the Bing Crosby generation is locked in the past, unwilling to admit that something newer may have merit. When I opined a couple of years ago that rap music is certainly not music by any definition I know, and I can't even understand what they are saying, one of my granddaughters smiled and said, "Granddaddy, that's a good thing!"

> "John the Baptist, chosen by God to prepare the way for Jesus, was such a bold and fearless proclaimer that he gave his life rather than abandon his principles."

Seeger songs like Where Have All the Flowers Gone?, If I Had a Hammer, and We Shall Overcome fueled a protest generation not always appreciated at the time but now recognized to have made lasting contributions to our history.

Life is divided into seasons – sometimes defined by the calendar, sometimes by nature, sometimes by emotion, sometimes by circumstances we can't control – but not everything in life is seasonal. Our service to God and humankind is a constant obligation and opportunity. That is no bargain-basement discipleship.

John the Baptist, chosen by God to prepare the way for Jesus, was such a bold and fearless proclaimer that he gave his life rather than abandon his principles. But there came a day when even John's certainty was tested while he languished in Herod's prison cell. He sent some followers to ask Jesus, "Are you the one who is to come, or should we expect someone else" (Matthew 11:3, (CSB)?

Resisting whatever inclination he might have had to display his divine credentials or assert his doctrinal and personal purity, Jesus chose to talk about his concern for people: "Go back and report to John what you have seen and heard:

> *The blind receive sight, the lame walk, those that have leprosy are cleansed, the deaf hear, the dead are raised, and the good news is proclaimed to the poor" (Luke 7:22, NIV).*

We can't do everything Jesus did, but we can give cups of cold water in his name, comfort those left battered and bleeding by the wayside, campaign for social justice, and see that the poor have the good news preached to them. That comes closer to reflecting the spirit of Christ than anything I can imagine.

We live in a time when words are plentiful, and deeds are scarce. The proper relationship between the two is captured in a statement attributed to St. Augustine: "Preach the gospel. If necessary, use words."

" *Redemption... is about the revival of a soul that was once dead*" (Rebekah Hallberg, Biblical Life Coach).

CHAPTER THIRTY-FIVE

The Man up Yonder Does Forgive

> *I'm almost embarrassed to tell you I used to be a preacher, because you just preached a better sermon than I ever did."*

The clerk at the pharmacy had just told me it would take a few more minutes to finish filling my prescriptions when she called the name of the man who walked up behind me and told him it would take a little longer for his as well. As he clapped a gnarled hand on my shoulder, he said, "It don't make no difference, and besides, this young feller here is ahead of me." As I turned to face him, I said, "Not any more I'm not; anybody who calls me young automatically goes to the head of the line!"

> *Dr. Floyd smiled, and gently said, 'It happened about 2,000 years ago on a hill called Calvary.'"*

As we moved to the chairs off to one side, he said, "Well, you may have me by a few years, but I've got you by a lot of miles."

Then he proceeded to tell me about his life as a construction worker, one who put up structural steel and operated a heavy crane. He told me how he got a broken arm, and why the fingers on one hand pointed in different directions. As he told me about some of the bad things he had done, he concluded, "If the man up yonder don't forgive me, I ain't got no hope." Then he said, "But you ain't told me what you used to do." "No," I said, "and I'm almost embarrassed to tell you I used to be a preacher, because you just preached a better sermon than I ever did: If the man up yonder doesn't forgive us, none of us have any hope."

In one of those strange happenings that we call coincidence but I think is often more, the very next morning when I opened my email there was a gracEmail message from my friend Edward Fudge, a Christian attorney in Houston, now deceased. He mentioned our mutual friend, Dr. Harvey Floyd, a Bible professor retired from Lipscomb University in Nashville. I graduated from Lipscomb in 1955, the same year Harvey returned to teach Bible and Greek. As Edward put it, that was the year that fortunate students "met a young new teacher named Harvey Floyd, who for the next two generations opened his Greek New Testament to Romans and Galatians, and God opened student hearts to see the Savior."

One of those students is now another Christian attorney in Houston, Mark Lanier. Mark remembers the day a student asked, "Dr. Floyd, please tell us about the day you got saved." Dr. Floyd smiled, and gently said, "It happened about 2,000 years ago on a hill called Calvary." Lanier remembers Floyd as a teacher who "always pointed us to Jesus' work."

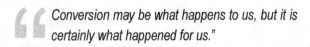
Conversion may be what happens to us, but it is certainly what happened for us."

Our salvation story is not always a dramatic Damascus road experience like the one Saul of Tarsus describes in Acts chapter nine in the New Testament. Conversion may not change us from Saul the Persecutor to Paul the Apostle, but it always changes us into "the image of his Son" (Romans 8:29, NASB).

Conversion may be what happens to us, but it is certainly what happened for us. It really is about what happened 2,000 years ago on a hill called Calvary.

Many people of New Testament times believed in multiple gods, all of whom had to be appeased, sometimes even with human sacrifices. They found it hard to believe in the one true God who turned things completely around and sacrificed himself for them.

> A cross was raised to silence the blasphemy that forgiveness is easy."

People of our day who have been imprisoned by performance-based religion also find it hard to believe that we can't earn God's favor. Jesus came to purchase our redemption, not to collect our dues.

Dietrich Bonhoeffer knew that people would find it hard to attach eternal value to a free gift, so he emphasized that what is free to us is costly to God. Grace is "costly because it cost God the life of his son: 'ye were bought at a price', and what has cost God much cannot be cheap for us. Above all, it is grace because God did not reckon his Son too dear a price to pay for our life but delivered him up for us. Costly grace is the Incarnation of God."

In contrast, "Cheap grace is the preaching of forgiveness without requiring repentance, baptism without church discipline, Communion without confession.... Cheap grace is grace without discipleship, grace without the cross, grace without Jesus Christ, living and incarnate." As George Buttrick said, "A cross was raised to silence the blasphemy that forgiveness is easy."

"Jesus paid it all; all to him I owe. Sin had left a crimson stain; he washed it white as snow." The man up yonder does forgive, my friend, and those are Encouraging Words!

CHAPTER THIRTY-SIX

God was There Every Single Time

> *The action still happens so fast that I can't begin to tell the difference between a triple Lutz and a triple toe loop."*

Unless your TV is broken or you are one of thousands still without power due to the winter storms where you live, you have probably spent some time recently watching the twenty-second (make that XXII) Winter Olympics. After the Olympic torch was set aflame in Greece, 14,000 torch bearers ran in relays 123 days carrying it some 40,000 miles, not counting the miles covered when it orbited the earth.

> *Carve ten minutes and twenty-seven seconds out of your day, go to www.youtube.com and find 'I Am Second,' Scott Hamilton's powerful testimony."*

Sochi, Russia was host city to the ninety-eight events in fifteen different winter sports. The NBC television network paid $775 million for the rights to televise the events, and who knows how much more for the actual production.

As usual, the most-watched events were the various women's figure skating displays of incredible balance, bodies that bend in impossible directions, and athletic flexibility beyond belief as the skaters glide with incredible grace over every inch of the 200' by 100' ice surface. The program calls them women, but most are teenage girls, some hardly meeting the age requirement. Despite the diagrams I've seen and the explanations I've heard, the action still happens so fast that I can't begin to tell the difference between a triple Lutz and a triple toe loop. But I trust Scott Hamilton's expert commentary.

For some of you who can remember things that happened thirty years ago, Scott Hamilton is still a story in his own right, or at least a story within a story. Competing at a robust 108 pounds on his five-foot-four-inch frame, Hamilton captured the hearts of a whole generation as he skated his way into both the U. S. Olympic and World Figure Skating Halls of Fame. In 1993, the Associated Press named Scott Hamilton one of the eight most popular athletes in America, ahead of other sports heroes like Michael Jordan, Magic Johnson, and Joe Montana.

This is the same Scott Hamilton who had stopped growing at two years of age, and after exhaustive tests was found to have a serious medical condition that could be treated with special diet and exercise. His big heart and unmatched determination carried him to sixteen consecutive national and world championships beginning in 1981. But the highlight of his career came in 1984 when he won the gold medal in men's figure skating at the Olympic Games in Sarajevo, Yugoslavia (now Bosnia-Herzegovina).

> *The same God who guided Scott through the tough spots has promised to be there for you as well, every single time, every single time."*

Maybe it's been thirty years since Scott won Olympic gold, but, at age fifty-four, bald head and all, he looks fit enough to do it again.

Scott's biggest battles and greatest victories were still to come. In 1997, he was diagnosed with testicular cancer, bad news for anybody but especially for a world-class athlete who longed for marriage and a family. In 2002 he and Tracie Robinson fell in love and married. Their answer-to-prayer son was born nine months and two days after their wedding day, a big win over testicular cancer. Scott and Tracie now have four children and live in Tennessee.

It was Tracie who helped Scott find the spiritual dimension in his life. She introduced him to my friend, Dr. Ken Durham, then at Pepperdine and now at Lipscomb University. Scott recalls the way Ken pointed him to the beginning of Christianity...how it is based on facts...real happenings. When Scott realized that the facts of the virgin birth, the life, the teachings, the miracles, and, ultimately, the sacrificial death and resurrection of Jesus called for a response on his part, he asked Ken to baptize him in the name of the Father, the Son, and the Holy Spirit, to wash away his sins in (where else?) Pepperdine's Olympic pool.

> When she took both his hands in hers and began to pray, Scott said he felt the peace and assurance of 'the most wonderful moment of my life....'"

A brain tumor, undiscovered earlier but present since birth, would test his faith through two surgeries. Scott remembers that awful day when he had to tell Tracie about the brain tumor. When she took both his hands in hers and began to pray, Scott said he felt the peace and assurance of "the most wonderful moment of my life.... I understood that through a strong relationship with Jesus you can endure anything.... God is there to guide you through the tough spots. God was there every single time, every single time."

Through my friend Dr. John Wilson at Pepperdine, I learned about something I want to share with you. Carve ten minutes and twenty-seven seconds out of your day, go to www.youtube.com and find "I Am Second," Scott Hamilton's powerful testimony. Have a box of tissues handy and watch another Gold Medal performance by a true Olympian. The same God who guided Scott through the tough spots has promised to be there for you as well, every single time, every single time.

CHAPTER THIRTY-SEVEN

A Smudge on Your Forehead

> He smiled, and gently said, 'I know; today is Ash Wednesday.'"

On a Wednesday, several years ago, I had a lunch appointment with an acquaintance who was not an intimate friend, but certainly not a stranger. As we waited for the hostess to prepare our table, I kept looking at him and wondering, do I tell him or just let it go? Finally deciding that a true friend would intervene, I leaned in close and said to him, "I don't want to meddle, but I also don't want you to be embarrassed; you have a dark smudge in the middle of your forehead." He smiled, and gently said, "I know; today is Ash Wednesday."

> I was so ignorant of Catholic teachings that I didn't even know what I didn't know."

Embarrassed? Not him, but me! Preacher man is supposed to know these things! I knew well the only Catholic family in our small town. Son Patrick was my age and a good friend – as good a friend as he could be going to a parochial school several miles away and shut out of community life. Every year or so when Patrick would get a new brother or sister, the rumors would start again: She is trying to have a dozen children because if she has twelve she will automatically become a saint, you know! No, I didn't know. In fact, I was so ignorant of Catholic teachings that I didn't even know what I didn't know.

All I really "knew" was that I should stay away from all things Catholic. No ashes on Wednesday, no fish on Friday. God forbid that anybody get the idea we might be like them. The one person in town always glad to see Patrick's mom was the manager of the Kroger store where I sacked groceries. It took several baskets, a few hundred dollars in a time when $20 bought a lot, and several trips to the family's station wagon to serve our star customer. Although I was curious, I was also polite, always inquiring about Patrick and his siblings. I managed to stay friendly with the family, and we learned from each other without corrupting each other.

Christians may draw strength from Ash Wednesday, Lent, Holy Week, Good Friday, or Easter without joining a particular tradition. In fact, I wonder why this holy season is not more widely celebrated. It takes some imagination to celebrate Christmas because we can't be sure December 25 is The Birthday. Easter is different in that the authenticity of the date is beyond question. The Council of Nicaea in 325 set a formula for determining the date for Easter, but, even before that, the relationship between Passover and Resurrection Sunday gave the day we call Easter its place in the calendar.

 Grace is scary because it appears to invite carelessness and disobedience."

Mardi Gras and Fat Tuesday are another matter. People who crave one last fling before committing themselves to forty days of fasting and prayer may be led by spirits, but not by The Spirit.

Catholics, with just one family and no parish in our little town, were an easy target for rumor, prejudice, and criticism. Ol' Pat's got it made. He can go out and do whatever he wants so long as he makes it back for Confession! We non-Catholics imagined, and perhaps longed for, a world where we also could sin without penalty if we prayed on schedule. We conveniently adopted the practice of claiming forgiveness that related to the opening prayer. Forgive me, Father, for I have sinned became Forgive us of all the sins we have committed since we last stood justified in thy sight. Bouncing from confession to confession is a lot like bouncing from prayer to prayer.

People who have looked for salvation by performance are understandably relieved to learn about grace and assurance. But grace is scary because it appears to invite carelessness and disobedience. The Apostle Paul knew that the idea of continual cleansing by the blood of Jesus (1 John 1:7, NASB) would tempt some of us to live with one foot in Christ and the other in the world. That heresy prompted him to ask and answer a most important question: "So what do we do? Keep on sinning so God can keep on forgiving? I should hope not!

> *Live like a sinner being cleansed by the blood, not like a sinner afraid to miss the next prayer!"*

"If we've left the country where sin is sovereign, how can we still live in our old house there? Or didn't you realize we packed up and left there for good? That is what happened in baptism. When we went under the water, we left the old country of sin behind; when we came up out of the water, we entered into the new country of grace – a new life in a new land" (Romans 6: 1-3, MSG)!

"Live like a sinner being cleansed by the blood, not like a sinner afraid to miss the next prayer!"

CHAPTER THIRTY-EIGHT

The Things of First Importance

> *At age thirty-three, his life is over, or, just beginning, depending on one's point of view."*

I suppose I was like all children in thinking Christmas is the most important day of the year. Then came 1941 when I learned some facts of life that destroyed my illusions. My new reality was that there is no once-for-all most important day. My birthday, the anniversary of my baptism, the day I got my driver's license, graduation day, wedding day, children's birthdays – all were important, even all-important at a given time.

> *He preached then, and underscored in his epistle, that the death, burial, and resurrection of Jesus are the things of 'first importance.'"*

Once again, we are at the point in our annual calendar when we remember the most important days of Jesus' life. Have you ever read a biography that had so many gaps in it? The story begins with his birth, then gets a little murky for a couple of years when the family escapes to Egypt, then grows dark as he grows up in Nazareth. He appears in public where, at the age of twelve, he astounds the elders with his knowledge of Torah. Then, silence again until the grown man appears at age thirty to demonstrate obedience to the Father by living and teaching the Father's will. At age thirty-three, his life is over, or, just beginning, depending on one's point of view.

> *Is it possible that the inspired authors of the four gospels passed over details of ordinary interest to focus on things of extraordinary interest?"*

Some biography! Out of a thirty-three-year life span we have snapshots from, what, five years? And details about a much shorter length of time? Could it be that the life of Jesus is told in such unconventional fashion because it was such an unconventional life? Is it possible that the inspired authors of the four gospels passed over details of ordinary interest to focus on things of extraordinary interest? The apostle Paul seems to suggest that when he writes to Christians in Corinth, "For what I received I passed on to you as of first importance: that Christ died for our sins according to the Scriptures, that he was buried, that he was raised on the third day according to the Scriptures, and that he appeared to Peter, and then to the Twelve…" (1 Corinthians 15: 3-5, NIV). Paul had visited Corinth at least twice, spending eighteen months there on his second mission journey. He preached then, and underscored in his epistle, that the death, burial, and resurrection of Jesus are the things of "first importance."

> *Twenty centuries have come and gone, and today He is the central figure of history, the leader of mankind's progress."*

No wonder the gospel writers placed such emphasis on the last days of Jesus' life! Some Bible scholars have estimated that fully a third of everything Matthew, Mark, Luke, and John wrote had to do with the last week of Jesus' life. Nineteenth-century Bible scholar J. W. McGarvey, harmonizing what he called "the fourfold gospel," said that, in the last week of his life, Jesus arrived in Bethany, just over the Mt. of Olives from Jerusalem, made his triumphal entry into Jerusalem on what we call Palm Sunday, pronounced a curse on a fig tree that bore no fruit, cleansed the temple, told parables about two sons, a wicked overseer, and the marriage of a king's son, answered questions about paying tribute to Caesar, discussed the resurrection with the Sadducees, answered a lawyer's question about the greatest commandment, preached his last public sermon, observed the generosity of a poor widow, dealt with Gentiles who wished to see Jesus, prophesied the destruction of Jerusalem, stressed the importance of living in a state of readiness, gave instructions for the preparation of the Passover meal, and suffered all the pain of betrayal, trial, and crucifixion. All in a single week!

In 1926, Dr. James Allan Francis tried to capture the significance of Jesus' life in a piece that has appeared in several prose and poetry collections under the heading One Solitary Life:

> *He was born in an obscure village, the child of a peasant woman. He grew up in still another village, where He worked in a carpenter shop until He was 30. Then for three years He was an itinerant preacher. He never wrote a book. He never held an office. He never had a family or owned a house. He didn't go to college. He never travelled more than 200 miles from the place He was born. He did none of the things one usually associates with greatness. He had no credentials*

but himself. He was only 33 when public opinion turned against him. His friends deserted him. He was turned over to His enemies and went through the mockery of a trial. He was nailed to a cross between two thieves. When He was dying, His executioners gambled for His clothing, the only property He had... on earth. When He was dead, He was laid in a borrowed grave through the pity of a friend. Twenty centuries have come and gone, and today He is the central figure of history, the leader of mankind's progress. All the armies that ever marched, all the navies that ever sailed, all the parliaments that ever sat, all the kings that ever reigned, put together, have not affected the life of man on earth as much as that One Solitary Life."

CHAPTER THIRTY-NINE

Blessed Assurance, Jesus Is Mine

> *The red chairs were supposed to be child-sized, but they were never my-sized."*

I can't remember a time when I didn't go to Sunday school and church. Nor can I remember a time when I didn't believe. And my memory goes all the way back to childhood in Mrs. Irma Graham's Sunday school class.

> *Mrs. Graham didn't have much training or much to work with, not even a flannel graph (ask your grandmother) but she had eternity in her heart."*

Her classroom had concrete block walls, a single light bulb hanging from the ceiling, an attendance chart with Jesus the Good Shepherd leaning over the edge of the cliff to rescue the little lamb in danger... and the red chairs. The red chairs were supposed to be child-sized, but they were never my-sized. I remember when my legs were so short my feet didn't touch the floor, and when my legs were so long my knees bumped my chin, but I don't remember an in-between time when the size was just right.

Mrs. Graham didn't have much training or much to work with, not even a flannel graph (ask your grandmother) but she had eternity in her heart. She loved her students, and she wanted us to love Jesus as much as she did. More important, she wanted us to know how much Jesus loved us.

I believed what Mrs. Graham taught because I knew she spoke with certainty rather than doubt. Why should I doubt what Mrs. Graham said the Bible said?

Questions came as I grew older and wondered how the Bible stories could be true. But I never quit believing because I never heard any alternative explanations that were more believable. The news this past week has described the "ripples" created by the "big bang" beginning of the universe 13.2 billion years ago. Is belief in that claim more certain than "In the beginning God…?" I'm not arguing with or disagreeing with the science, but I am saying that both explanations require faith. The discoveries of science won't allow me to accept a "young earth" theory, and they certainly don't require me to accept the calculations of seventeenth century Bishop James Ussher who claimed that creation occurred at the beginning of the night which preceded the 23rd of October in the year 710 of the Julian period, or 4004 B. C. Embracing faith does not require endorsing faulty scholarship.

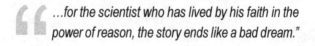
> …for the scientist who has lived by his faith in the power of reason, the story ends like a bad dream."

An organization called Mars One announced plans to send humans on a one-way trip to Mars by 2023. More than 200,000 people volunteered to go and die, and 1,058, including 297 from the United States, have made the first cut. A man whose wife is still in the running said he loved her so much he would support her decision. Yet people call our faith in the Bible foolish!

Several years before his death in 2008, Dr. Robert Jastrow, an astronomer and physicist, graciously gave me permission to reprint an article from his book, *God and the Astronomer*. Dr. Jastrow, who earned a Ph.D. in theoretical physics from Columbia University and joined NASA when it was formed in 1958, described himself as "agnostic, not a believer." Yet he wrote:

> At this moment it seems as though science will never be able to raise the curtain on the mystery of creation. For the scientist who has lived by his faith in the power of reason, the story ends like a bad dream. He has scaled the mountains of ignorance; he is about to conquer the highest peak; as he pulls himself over the final rock, he is greeted by a band of theologians who have been sitting there for centuries."

That's not to say that theologians are smarter than scientists. It is to say that truth may be found in more than one discipline, and that truth may be revealed as well as discovered. Nobody believes nothing; everybody believes something. Even the person who professes not to believe believes in his non-belief.

On the cross, Jesus gave up his life, fully aware that if God left him in the tomb there would be no other way to escape the tomb. Jesus believed what his followers found hard to believe: his tomb would be empty on Easter morning.

> Even the person who professes not to believe believes in his non-belief."

A dear Christian friend died yesterday, just a few weeks short of her ninety-sixth birthday. She slipped into eternity with her three sons and their families softly singing to her, "Blessed assurance, Jesus is mine…."

I've lived a long time with that assurance, and I have no reason now to stop believing those Encouraging Words.

CHAPTER FORTY

I Will Never Leave you nor Forsake you

> "We were almost afraid to take a bath because water and polio were rumored to go together."

The summer of 1941 was ideal for an eight-year-old boy. School was out and the weather was nice so I could play outside with my friends every day. I was vaguely aware that my mother and daddy were talking about the Great Depression finally being over, but that meant nothing to me. And if they had any fears of the gathering clouds of war, that was no concern of mine. At that point I didn't even know I would have a baby brother before the end of the year.

> "She never got over that grief, nor did she get past her resentment of mothers like mine who still had their sons."

My summer was ideal… until boys and girls my age began getting sick with the dreaded polio virus. Although it would not make a huge impact nationally until a few years later, polio seemed especially vicious in our small town where everybody knew everybody.

My summer became very different. Parents were afraid to let their children play with other children. The community swimming pool closed, as did the movie theater. No more squirting playmates with the hose. We were almost afraid to take a bath because water and polio were rumored to go together. And rumor was what fueled our fears in that pre-television era when most people didn't even have telephones. Have you heard that the Smith boy will have to wear leg braces in order to stand or walk? No, but I heard that the Jones girl will have to be in an iron lung the rest of her life.

> *Comfort has come, not so much from the 'pretty' scriptures like the twenty-third Psalm, but from the anguish of people who grieved as we have."*

It was no rumor when my mother told me that my friend Billy had polio. I remember how somber my mother was when she told me that news, and how she wept a few days later when she told me Billy had died. I didn't know anything about death, except that Billy wouldn't be there anymore. I was ready to do my grieving and get on with my life. But Billy's mother wasn't ready to let that happen. I'll never forget the Sunday at church when she took my face in her two hands and almost screamed, "Why did God take my Billy and let you live? Why? Why? Just tell me why!" You may think that was an unbelievably cruel thing for an adult to do to a child, but Mrs. Boatman was not a cruel woman. She was a loving mother grieving the loss of her only child. She never got over that grief, nor did she get past her resentment of mothers like mine who still had their sons.

> *There is a reason why a whole book in the Bible is called Lamentations."*

I've understood Billy's mother a whole lot better this past year because I have been in God's face many times. If I could have held his face between my hands and screamed at him, I would have demanded, "Just tell me why!" You see, just a year ago Keith Kreidel, more son than son-in-law, died of a stroke suffered four days earlier. A good man in the prime of life, physically fit, active... a loving husband and father... Why? Why would such a man suffer a combination of catastrophic events a doctor described as "the perfect storm?" We have been paralyzed by our grief, unable to comfort our daughter and our grandchildren.

> *Job was not one to say, 'Why me?' His attitude was Why not me?"*

Comfort has come, not so much from the "pretty" scriptures like the twenty-third Psalm, as from the anguish of people who grieved as we have. There is a reason why a whole book in the Bible is called Lamentations. "Is any suffering like my suffering that was inflicted on me...? (Lamentatioins 1:12, NIV)? People turn to the Psalms for comfort, but when David bares his soul we realize we are kindred spirits. "How long, O Lord? Will you forget me forever? How long will you hide your face from me?" (Psalm 13:1, NIV). "My God, my God, why have you forsaken me?... O my God, I cry out by day, but you do not answer..." (Psalm 22:1, 2, NIV).

> *When God chose Joshua to succeed Moses as the leader of his people, he gave a promise that he still honors: 'I will never leave you nor forsake you. Be strong and courageous....'" (Joshua 1:9, NIV).*

I don't pretend to understand the Old Testament book of Job. God allowed this "blameless and upright" man to suffer at the hand of Satan until his possessions, his sons and daughters, and even his health were taken away. Job's three friends were convinced he had committed some secret sin for which he was being punished. For Job's wife, suffering along with her husband, the easy way out was to "Curse God and die!" (Job 2: 9, NIV). But Job was not one to say, "Why me?" His attitude was Why not me? "Shall we accept good from God, and not trouble? (Job 2: 10, NIV). From beginning to end he was sustained by his faith: "The Lord gave and the Lord has taken away; may the name of the Lord be praised" (Job 1: 21, NIV).

If Billy's mom were still alive, I would say to her, "I couldn't answer your question when I was an eight-year-old boy, and now that I'm an eighty-year-old man I still can't. But I can tell you that when God chose Joshua to succeed Moses as the leader of his people, he gave a promise that he still honors: 'I will never leave you nor forsake you. Be strong and courageous...'" (Joshua 1: 5, 6, NIV).

CPSIA information can be obtained
at www.ICGtesting.com
Printed in the USA
LVHW040235161220
674283LV00001B/1